Beating the Market, 3 Months at a Time

Beating the Market, 3 Months at a Time

3 Months at a Time

A Proven Investing Plan Everyone Can Use

Gerald Appel ■ Marvin Appel

Vice President, Publisher: Tim Moore
Associate Publisher and Director of Marketing: Amy Neidlinger
Executive Editor: Jim Boyd
Editorial Assistant: Pamela Boland
Development Editor: Russ Hall
Digital Marketing Manager: Julie Phifer
Marketing Coordinator: Megan Colvin
Cover Designer: Alan Clements
Managing Editor: Gina Kanouse
Senior Project Editor: Kristy Hart
Copy Editor: Water Crest Publishing
Proofreader: Williams Woods Publishing
Indexer: Erika Millen
Compositor: codeMantra
Manufacturing Buyer: Dan Uhrig

Pearson Education LTD.
Pearson Education Australia PTY, Limited.
Pearson Education Singapore, Pte. Ltd.
Pearson Education North Asia, Ltd.
Pearson Education Canada, Ltd.
Pearson Educatión de Mexico, S.A. de C.V.
Pearson Education—Japan
Pearson Education Malaysia, Pte. Ltd.

Library of Congress Cataloging-in-Publication Data

Appel, Gerald.

Beating the market, 3 months at a time : a proven investing plan everyone can use/Gerald Appel, Marvin Appel.

p. cm.

ISBN 0-13-613089-5 (hardback : alk. paper) 1. Investments. 2. Speculation. 3. Portfolio management. I. Appel, Marvin. II. Title.

HG4521.A637 2008

332.6--dc22

2007036329

To our wife and mother, Judith Appel, for all the love
and support she has provided to both of us
over all these years.

Contents

Acknowledgments

We would like to acknowledge the many market analysts from whom we have learned over the years and all of the useful Internet websites associated with the stock and other investment markets that contribute to our knowledge day by day. In particular, we would like to cite the contributions of Yale and Jeffrey Hirsch to the study of seasonal factors that influence the stock market and of Ned Davis, whose work covers such a broad scope.

We also wish to acknowledge the assistance of the research and portfolio staffs of Signalert Corporation and of Appel Asset Management Corporation—Glenn Gortler, Arthur Appel, Joon Choi, Roni Greiff Nelson, Bonnie Gortler, Joanne Quan Stein, among others. Their editorial and research contributions were invaluable in the research that went into this work as well as in its written preparation.

Our thanks as well to the editorial staff at FT Press for their encouragement, support, and suggestions all of which helped us prepare what we hope is a readable and useful work.

We do trust that readers do not find difficulty in dealing with what may well appear to be two distinct styles of writing among the various chapters in the book, which were written separately by the authors although the content represents, for the very most part, a joint effort.

Gerald Appel
Marvin Appel

About the Authors

Dr. Marvin Appel is CEO of Appel Asset Management Corporation and Vice President of Signalert Corporation, Registered Investment Advisors in Great Neck, New York, which together manage more than $300 million for individual clients. He also edits the highly acclaimed investment newsletter, *Systems and Forecasts,* and has authored *Investing with Exchange Traded Funds Made Easy* (FT Press, 2006).

He has been featured on CNNfn, CNBC, CBS Marketwatch.com, and Forbes.com, and has presented at conferences ranging from the World Series of Exchange Traded Funds to the American Association of Individual Investors. The New York State Legislature has invited Dr. Appel to present his economic and investment outlook.

Gerald Appel is a world famous author and lecturer. A frequent guest on television and radio, he has appeared on Wall Street Week with Louis Ruykeyser and his articles and/or articles about him have appeared in *Money Magazine, Barron's, Technical Analysis of Stocks and Commodities Magazine, Stocks Futures and Options Magazine, Wealth Magazine,* the *New York Times, Forbes, Kiplinger's Magazine,* and elsewhere. He is the founder of Signalert Corporation, an investment advisory firm that manages more than $300 million in client assets and is the author of numerous books and articles regarding investment strategies, including *Technical Analysis: Power Tools for the Active Investor* (Financial Times Prentice Hall, 2005).

Introduction _____

"Financial Savvy"
How To Invest Smart So You Will Have
the Money You Need When You Need It

By Gerald Appel and Dr. Marvin Appel

Articles and discussions of financial and investment planning generally focus on the accumulation of assets for the later stages of life—to provide for the maintenance of standards of living, medical needs, creation of estates, and vacations.

Each period of life carries with it special financial requirements associated with that particular stage. In certain ways, young adults require less capital than older adults. Medical expenses tend to be considerably lower. Younger people are more capable of traveling "on the cheap," in hostels, camping, and in less luxurious and/or group accommodations. They are usually more able to share apartments, to live in relatively small quarters.

On the other hand, younger people also often find themselves in situations that call for unusually large expenditures. New businesses and professional practices require start-up capital. Living accommodations have become particularly expensive in major cities across America. Funds may be needed to pay off college loans, perhaps to finance graduate school and other forms of advanced education. Certain professions, such as medicine, require long training periods, which may coincide with marriage and even with parenthood.

The age period between, perhaps, 33–45 is usually a period of increasing professional accomplishment and rising income. It is also a period of sharply rising expenses to meet the needs of growing families, which may require larger homes, multiple automobiles, summer camp, family vacations, perhaps private school, payment for special child events, and a whole multitude of expenses that families assume to be certain that their children have what other children have.

This is also the period during which families attempt to set aside the money needed to finance college, weddings, and other expenses incurred by children as they move through adolescence into young adulthood.

Although investment programs are best initiated as early in life as possible, it is not surprising that for many couples and individuals, serious capital accumulation tends to start only after the children, if any, have left the house. Fortunately, for most people, peak earnings often take place at this time. Hopefully, the years between middle age and retirement prove sufficient for the accumulation of capital needed later on.

Financial Planning and Sharp Investing Are Not Just for the Older Folk...

What is the point of all this discussion, which really, if we think about it, contains few surprises?

Well, you can work hard throughout your life to make the money you need to keep up with life's changing needs. Or, you can try to plan and carry through your affairs so that you accumulate an amount of money along the way that, by savvy, active investing, *you can make work for you!*

Which Is Where This Book Comes In...

It is, of course, possible to hand over your assets to a financial planner or to a money manager or to a stock broker (in recent years, referred to as an investment consultant) or to a mutual fund family, to step aside, and to hope for the best. Many managers have had excellent long-term performance records, and some will even make a reasonably serious attempt to match the portfolios they create for you to your own personal life situation, risk tolerances, and temperament.

Why and How to Become a Self-Sufficient Investor

However, although there are definite potential benefits that can accrue from retaining professional managers, there are also some definite disadvantages. For one, the use of professional managers usually involves additional expenses for your investment portfolio—typical management fees ranging between 1–2% of assets per annum, depending upon the size of your account. Hedge funds generally charge much higher management fees.

In many cases, professional money managers bring with them potential conflicts of interest in one form or another. Insurance agents, mutual fund managers, and brokerage house personnel work for and are paid by their companies whose interests often take precedence over the interests of customers. For example, financial advisors and/or brokerage house personnel often receive commission income paid by mutual funds to them for the products they recommend and sell, as well as management or custodian fees from client customers for as long as accounts stay open. It can be readily understood that such commissions are likely to impact the recommendations made by such advisors, particularly when alternative investment choices might lie with mutual funds that pay no commissions whatsoever to salespeople.

Investment representatives, brokers, or managers associated with large brokerage houses, mutual funds, banks, or other financial institutions may or may not have the ability to distinguish between "safe" market periods and unsafe periods. They may or may not even have the discretion within their firms to advise clients regarding market conditions. Would it really be possible for an employee of a large brokerage house to advise his clients to liquidate equity positions and to move totally or near totally into cash? Could and would any major brokerage house urge its clientele as a group to sharply reduce their stock holdings? Could or would a major mutual fund family urge shareholders to redeem shares of its mutual funds because of negative market prospects?

Not very likely. Financial institutions rarely emphasize selling strategies. Wall Street emphasizes buying rather than selling recommendations. (It is not necessarily generally understood, but on Wall Street, when investment analysts become negative on a particular company, they do not downgrade its rating from "buy" to "sell" but rather from "buy" to "hold," which sounds like an entirely different opinion unless you are familiar with the code.)

You might just try to tune into one or the other of the television channels that specialize in tracking the stock market. Compare the number of times guests are asked to suggest stocks to sell compared to the number of times that they are asked to suggest stocks to buy.

Neither last nor least, brokerage houses, wealth managers, asset managers, and financial planners are most likely to provide careful supervision to "wealth assets," usually thought of as clients who have at least one million dollars worth of assets in account. The odds are much less that clients with relatively small amounts of assets—small to wealth managers, that is, but significant to these clients—will receive careful supervision, monitoring, and general attention.

To Sum Up the Alternatives

The hiring of professional investment managers may secure for investors useful general financial planning assistance, useful professional investment advice, and at least a modicum of personalized supervision of investment assets.

That said, professional investment advice is often tainted by conflicts of interest, well meaning but not necessarily superior investment guidance, and possibly by some neglect of your own particular individual investment portfolios.

In any event, if you ultimately choose to delegate the task of managing your investments to others, choose your managers with care, taking care to verify their actual long-term performance with other accounts, and particularly their ability to protect assets during poor as well as favorable general stock market and economic climates. At the very least, learn enough to be able to evaluate the strategies that are being employed on your behalf.

What You Will Learn from This Work

You may or may not have the desire or time to "do it all yourself." However, we have designed this book to provide you with specific, well-researched tools that you may well employ in self-directed investment programs to grow your assets and to build a way of life that will benefit you and yours for possibly decades to come.

More specifically, you will learn techniques by which you can increase the safety of your stock and bond investment instruments and how to manage your investment portfolio to improve your rates of return while reducing risk. You will learn how to identify those market sectors that are leading and likely to continue to lead in strength. You will learn when and why to buy short-term bonds and when and why to switch to the longer-term side of the bond market. You will learn how and when to invest in emerging markets, such as Brazil and India, and when to concentrate in longer-established stock markets, such as Europe and the United States. You will learn when to buy large and well-established companies in basic industries and when to buy into newly emerging corporations.

We will start with some investment basics, underlying principles of successful investing that are strongly recommended. You will learn a number of specific strategies that you can put to work immediately to grow your assets over the years, strategies that will provide for you specific times to enter and specific times to exit investment positions. Finally, you explore some unpleasant facts of economic life for motivational purposes, move from there into setting accumulation targets— hopefully realistic goals that are compatible with your personal economic situation.

The strategies that you will learn have been well researched, and though they require little time to apply (often no more than one hour every three months), they are likely to increase your investment returns significantly while reducing risks associated with buying, hoping, and holding.

If you are able to maintain investment discipline, to put a certain amount of time into the project, and to enjoy rather than fear decision making, you may well find your long-term growth of capital to be gratifying indeed. This is in addition to the satisfaction of knowing what you have personally accomplished for yourself and your family over the years involved.

We believe that this book provides the useful tools you need. The rest will be up to you....

1

Putting Together a Winning Investment Portfolio

Rather than to extend our introductions, we will move immediately into specific basic and advanced concepts regarding the establishment and maintenance of investment portfolios. Specifically, in chapters to come, you will examine various forms that income investments may take and ways and means of profiting from such investments. You will learn basic and advanced concepts relating to income investing, how to achieve profit in various investment climates, as well as how to reduce risk.

The Stock Market Will Not Be Neglected...

You will also be exploring issues such as the construction of stock portfolios—the benefits of diversification and active portfolio re-allocation strategies. You will learn methods of selecting mutual funds most likely to succeed and ways to make use of "exchange traded funds"—exciting, recently introduced investment vehicles that provide the means of creating portfolios that may be balanced by geography, by industry, by market sector, and by investment objective.

1

You will learn specific strategies that have been designed to produce higher rates of return than random selection, with the benefits of risk reduction as well.

By this time, you should have secured a sufficient arsenal of strategies to provide tools you will require for long-term investment success.[1]

The Key Elements of Your Winning Investment Portfolio

Investment portfolios—which should be thought of as flexible, dynamic, and responsive to changes in investment climates—should have three characteristics, as follows:

- Balance
- Diversification
- The ability to outperform its component benchmarks

Let's consider these in order.

Balance

Portfolios should be "balanced" in a number of ways. Their composition should include components whose major objectives lie in the area of income production, the provision of a consistent stream of income that might consist of bond interest and dividends, as well as prospects of capital gain from stock and bond market-related positions.

The various forms of stocks, bonds, mutual funds, and exchange traded funds represent different areas of investment with varying investment objectives, each of which carries its own levels of risk and profit potential.

Diversification

Diversification involves the construction of your investment portfolio so that the portfolio's components represent different areas of investment, which tend to rise and to fall at different times, with differing risk-reward patterns. These characteristics will tend to smooth the performance of your portfolio, reducing risk considerably while actually benefiting performance.

For example, REITs—real estate trusts that invest in real estate holdings of various sorts—tend to produce, over the years, rates of return that are essentially similar to rates of return produced by portfolios of stocks that might be representative of the Standard & Poor's 500 Index, a generally employed benchmark of stock market performance.

Although rates of return of REITs and the Standard & Poor's 500 Index have been similar over the long run, REITs tend to move independently of other stock market groups, frequently rising when most other industry groups decline, and often declining when most other industry groups are advancing in price. REITs may be said to be uncorrelated rather than correlated with most of the rest of the stock market.

As you might expect, a portfolio consisting of 50% of REITs and 50% of the Standard & Poor's 500 Index will tend to be more consistent in its performance than a portfolio consisting solely of one or the other. Losses are generally more contained in diversified than in undiversified portfolios at no penalty to performance.

Diversification, which is related to balance, may involve diversification between stocks and bonds, between stocks in large companies and smaller company stocks, between domestic corporations and overseas equities, between different types of bonds, and between income-oriented equities and growth stocks.

Commodity-Based Investments as a Hedge Against Inflation

There is one area of investment opportunity that we have not yet mentioned—the potential for investments in commodities such as raw materials, gold, oil and other energy products, food, and agriculture. It is possible to invest directly in such vehicles by way of futures contracts, but it is also possible to invest indirectly in such arenas through the stock market by utilizing exchange traded funds (ETFs), stocks, and mutual funds.

Commodities tend to rise in price during periods of high inflation. Rising prices tend to result in reductions in the prices of bonds since the fixed interest rate returns from bonds tend to be less attractive in climates of rising inflation. Stocks tend to benefit from moderate inflationary pressures but not from rampant price rises.

The prices of gold, silver, palladium, and aluminum tend to rise rapidly during periods of inflation—such as during early 1980, when the price of gold reached $800 per ounce, bond yields approached 15%, and stocks fell under a cloud. Pressures on both the bond and stock markets have occurred since then during various energy and other commodity crises, to the benefit of commodity-related investments.

A certain amount of commodity representation may be well advised in most diversified portfolios.

Outperformance

You will, of course, want the components of your portfolio to outperform their peers. If you invest in mutual funds, you will want to own mutual funds whose long-term and/or intermediate-term (several months) performances are above average. You will want to place capital invested in stocks into individual issues and industry groups that are leading in market performance and to be prepared to exit positions when their leadership wanes.

As we move along, you will learn specific, well-researched, and time-proven strategies that you may apply in a consistent manner to achieve outperformance compared to the average investment of similar risk.

Goals

These might seem somewhat self-evident, but your goals in the creation of your investment portfolios are as follows:

1. To secure rates of return superior to those that might be achieved by risk-free investments such as money market funds or 90-day treasury bills.
2. To learn which rates of return should meet your financial goals if you were to extrapolate the growth of your investment portfolio during the periods over which you expect to be invested.
3. To maintain risk at acceptable levels.

Risk Levels Associated with Investments of Varying Investment Objectives

As a general rule, investments made for the purposes of consistent and predictable income, particularly if they are made in higher-quality areas (such as prime bonds or treasury issues), carry less risk than investments made in the stock market. Higher dividend-paying stocks tend to carry less risk than speculative growth stocks. Mutual funds that invest in value-oriented securities generally carry less risk than mutual funds that invest in more speculative technologies while, at the same time, actually producing higher average rates of long-term return than more volatile growth funds.

As an example of the relationships that have historically existed between risk and reward, you might consider the following blends of holdings in the Standard & Poor's 500 Index and intermediate United States Government bonds (see Table 1.1).

TABLE 1.1 Rates of Return and Risk Levels, Stock-Bond Portfolio Allocations
Stocks—Standard & Poor's 500 Index, Bonds—U.S. Intermediate Government

		Annual Returns		
Percent Stocks	Percent Bonds	Highest	Average	Lowest
100	0	+41.1%	+10.3%	-24.9%
90	10	+38.9	+10.2	-23.3
80	20	+34.4	+ 9.9	-20.0
70	30	+31.2	+ 9.6	-16.8
60	**40**	**+29.2**	**+ 9.3**	**-13.6**
50	50	+27.1	+ 8.9	-10.4
40	60	+26.0	+ 8.6	- 7.2
30	70	+26.8	+ 8.1	- 4.0
20	80	+27.6	+ 7.7	- 3.9
10	90	+28.3	+ 7.2	- 4.5
0	100	+29.1	+ 6.8	- 5.1

Source: Sit Investment Associates from Ibbotson Presentation Materials © 2006 Ibbotson Associates, Inc. Period covered: 1956–2005.

Observations

Although U.S. intermediate treasury bonds are among the most conservative of investments, their inclusion in a balanced stock-bond portfolio does not greatly impact the average annual return of an all-stock portfolio but can reduce the maximum risk considerably.

For example, the establishment of a 60% stock–40% bond portfolio as compared to an all-stock portfolio reduced the average annual rate of return from 10.3% to 9.3% but also reduced the worst-year risk from 24.9% to just 13.6%. Best-year results were reduced from 41.1% to 29.2%.

By initiating a balance in your portfolio, you would have reduced your risk by nearly one-half while reducing your annual rate of return by just one percent per year. Would stocks alone provide the greater return over the long run? Yes. But would you be able to absorb a loss of as much as 24.9% in just one year, a loss of over 45% over a span of two to three years (2000–2002)? Would you especially be able to absorb such a loss if, at the same time, you were drawing from your account for living expenses, where such withdrawals would deplete the assets remaining for growth in the future?

The Preferred Mix for Most Investors

Most investors are probably best off with a stock-bond portfolio balanced somewhere between 80–20% and 60–40%, stocks to bonds, but blends that include as little as 20% stocks still add performance to bond-only portfolios with even less risk than bonds alone involve.

How Do You Decide on Your Blend?

Your first step is to appraise your own financial and temperamental abilities to accept loss.

If you are relatively young with many productive work years ahead of you, you may be able to afford risks involved in a portfolio that is heavily concentrated in stocks that would be likely, over the long run, to produce the highest rates of return.

As time passes, you would probably want to reduce risk as your assets grow sufficiently to meet your projected retirement and other needs. (No need to risk a solid financial foundation.) If your asset base is borderline in terms of your expenses as life passes along, it would probably be a better idea to try to reduce spending rather than to accept higher levels of risk. The bear market that started in 2000 and which did not end until 2003 produced losses of more than 75% for investors in the Nasdaq Composite and more than 45% for investors in the Standard & Poor's 500 Index, in addition to which many retirees were drawing on diminishing assets for living expenses.

This, and other periods (such as 1973–1974), were calamitous for speculative investments. The preservation of needed capital should be a major criterion in making investment decisions.

THE GREATEST MISTAKE YOU CAN MAKE IN THE STOCK MARKET IS TO TAKE A LARGER LOSS THAN YOU CAN AFFORD!

"He Who Fights and Runs Away Lives to Fight Another Day..."

What did Cisco, Oracle, and Lucent have in common?

These were all stocks that were hot, cooled off, and left thousands and thousands of investors holding the bag when their collapses came. As a general rule, "hot" stocks attract the most interest near their peak price levels. In any event, even if you happen to pass over what turn out to be attractive opportunities, you will probably still have your capital, and other opportunities do arise.

But What Happens if You Lose?

Well, if you take a 50% loss in your asset base, you will need to make 100% on your remaining capital just to get even. (It does not matter whether you first make the 100% and then lose 50% of your assets or the other way around. For every 50% you lose, you will need a profit of 100% just to break even.)

For every 25% you lose, you will need to make 33% to get even. For example, if you start with $100 and lose $25, leaving you with $75, you will need to make $25 on the remaining $75 to bring you back to your starting amount, $100.

Unless you are relatively early in the period in which you are accumulating capital, and absolutely able and willing to accept the risks involved, do not invest without carefully assessing the impact of potential losses. This is more important than assessing the glory of potential gain. For many, if not most, investors, the investment game is as much about "feeling smart" as about making money. (Feeling smart is not necessarily the same as being smart.) Risk control, again, is a vital portion of investment planning.

Just to Restate...

Your primary goal as an investor is to achieve an amount of assets that you will require to meet life expenses—throughout your life—but particularly later in life when work income comes to an end or is, at the least, reduced.

You can achieve your goals by way of astute investing, which usually involves diversification, diversification, and more diversification and portfolio balance.

Diversification will help reduce risk. You should, nonetheless, be prepared to rapidly exit positions that are not performing as you expect.

As a general rule, the best losses are those losses that are taken quickly.

Making money is not about feeling smart. Making money is about disciplined portfolio management, the ability to invest against the crowd, and the ability to retain emotional and portfolio balance.

In the next chapter, you will explore the world of bond investing. Before you do, however, here is just one final review of some of the concepts basic to profitable investment.

Portfolio Composition

Investments are made in the stock market primarily for capital gain, although certain classes of stock do provide significant streams of income. Stocks are intrinsically more speculative than investment grade bonds, but have, in the past, generally produced higher rates of return to investors.

Investments are made in bonds primarily for predictable streams of interest income, although capital gains or losses may develop as, respectively, interest rates decline or rise.

Commodity-related investments are most likely to produce profit during periods of high inflation when both stocks and bonds may fall under price pressure.

Portfolios should be well diversified based upon geography, the structure of the investment, industry, and risk level.

It is better to miss a profit than to take a loss.

How to Gauge Prospects for the Stock Market by Checking Out the CRB Index of Commodity Prices[2]

There have been, in recent years, upsurges in the prices of many commodities, including oil, gold, agricultural products, and industrial and precious metals, among other raw materials. Moreover, with the expansion of the economies of many countries abroad, demand for raw materials appears likely to increase. The question for investors is: "Are surges in commodity prices likely to have beneficial or negative effects on stock prices?" This article will address the past history of stock market behavior in relationship to the direction of commodity price movement, with conclusions based on studies covering the period from February 1973 to January 2006.

The Commodity Research Bureau (www.crbtrader.com) maintains the CRB Index of Commodity Prices, an index that includes seventeen individual commodity futures prices representing a number of various commodity sectors. The index is posted on an intra-day and daily basis, available on the preceding website and elsewhere.

A study of the relationships between stock prices and the movement of the CRB Index, 1973–January 2006, reveals the following relationships, expressed in Figure 1.1.

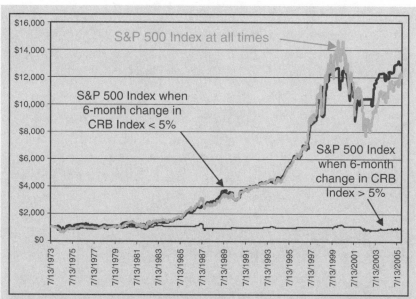

During periods of high inflation, the Standard & Poor's 500 Index grew at a rate of 0.4% while invested. During lower-inflation periods, the Standard & Poor's 500 Index grew at a rate of 11.7% per year. All periods included, the Standard & Poor's 500 Index advanced at a rate of 8% per year.

Figure 1.1 Growth in the S & P 500 Index during periods of high versus low rates of commodity price inflation (1973–2006)

The Study and Results

Rates of inflation were derived by measuring changes in the levels of the CRB Index over periods of six months—the latest reading compared to readings six months previous. Rates of inflation were considered high when the index advanced by 5% or more (for example, from 200 to 210 or from 100 to 105). Rates of inflation were considered to be relatively low when increases in the CRB Index over six-month periods were less than 5%. Gains and losses in the Standard & Poor's 500 Index were measured monthly, with periods categorized into high-inflation and low-inflation climates.

Inflation Is Bad for the Stock Market!

As you can see in Figure 1.1, higher levels of inflation are bad for the stock market, as well as for bonds.

During periods of high inflation (lowest price scale on the chart), which prevailed 32% of the time during the 1973–2006 time span covered, the Standard & Poor's 500 Index advanced at a rate of just 0.4% per annum.

During periods of low inflation (middle scale), stocks advanced at a rate of 11.7% per year.

Taking all periods together, the Standard & Poor's 500 Index advanced at a rate of 8% per year. This is the upper scale, which includes gains achieved during both high-inflation and low-inflation periods.

Inflation Has Been Bad for Stocks Overseas as Well

A review of price movements of stocks of countries abroad indicates that similar patterns apply to international as to domestic stock markets. Almost all gains that have taken place in the EAFE (Europe, Australia, Far East) Index have taken place during periods of no or low inflation in commodity prices.

Value Stocks Do Better Than Growth Stocks When Inflationary Pressures Are High!

Value-oriented, large company stocks fare relatively well compared to growth companies during periods of sharply rising commodity prices.

This is not surprising when we consider the fact that most energy-related companies such as oil producers, refineries, and drillers are large, value-oriented companies that prosper from rising energy prices. The same might be said for companies such as Alcoa, which produces aluminum. Growth companies, more likely to consume than to produce commodities, do not fare as well during periods of high inflation.

Summing Up

Although correlations are not perfect, it does appear clear that investors in both overseas and domestic securities are more likely to prosper during periods of relative price stability than during periods of rising commodity prices. Differences in the performance of the stock market between high inflationary periods and periods of relatively low inflation have been significant over the years, certainly of a magnitude to warrant the ongoing tracking of this indicator.

2

Advanced Diversification and Risk Management

In Chapter 1, "Putting Together a Winning Investment Portfolio," you considered the concept of diversification, and ways in which proper portfolio diversification can provide additional profit while reducing risk. In this chapter, you examine certain active procedures associated with proper diversification, look at a sample diversified portfolio, explore some different ways of recognizing risks associated with investment positions, and consider the structure of investment vehicles, mutual funds, and exchange traded funds (ETFs) that you may want to employ as your investment vehicles.

An Example of Well-Balanced Diversification

A well-diversified portfolio consists of segments of investments that are "uncorrelated"—that is, not particularly likely to rise and to fall at the same time. Although there are times when just about all segments of such portfolios may move in tandem, as often as not they may rise and fall independently of each other, so that performance of the portfolio as a whole is smoother than the performance of each segment alone, as gains in winning sectors may be offset by losses elsewhere, and losses in losing sectors will be offset by gains in winning sectors.

Portfolio Diversification Based on Industry Sector and Geography

Diversified portfolios may be created in many ways. For example, the following blend of industry and geographically based holdings should provide, in the future as in the past, the benefits of diversification. Furthermore, investments in the following areas may be readily made via mutual funds and/or exchange traded funds:

- **Investments in the financial industry.** The financial sector of the stock market—which includes insurance, banking, and brokerage houses, as well as related industries—has been among the strongest of stock market sectors. The performance of this industry tends to correlate closely with market indices, such as the Standard & Poor's 500 Index that reflects major, well-established, corporations.

- **Utilities.** In the past, a somewhat more conservative than average market sector. Many utility issues pay higher than average dividends and are often preferred by conservative, income-oriented investors. Nonetheless, this sector is subject to serious market decline from time to time, especially when interest rates are rising. In recent years, the industry's fortunes have been increasingly tied to energy prices, with certain sectors of the industry benefiting when energy prices in general rise.

- **Real Estate Investment Trusts (REITs).** You considered this industry sector in Chapter 1. REITs belong in virtually all well-diversified portfolios. The performance of this industry sector has been roughly equal to the performance of the financial sectors over the past decade or so, but real estate has, during this period, been more stable.

- **Energy.** Includes oil producers, drilling companies, oil shipping, coal producers, and related industries. At this time, a good hedge against inflation and against certain forms of international difficulties. In recent years, an outstanding performing sector.

- **Materials.** Industries associated with gold, silver, lumber, various minerals, and related industries. A good hedge against inflation, these sectors often advance in price at times when inflationary pressures adversely affect other industry groups.

- **U.S. small-capitalization value sectors.** Many of the industries cited previously are likely to be represented by major, larger capitalization companies. Smaller companies whose price represents current value and earnings have performed well historically and often at times that larger capitalization companies do not.

- **International equities.** Markets overseas have been gaining in strength relative to the United States market in recent years and also growing in size in comparison to the United States stock market. Geographical diversification is recommended and will be further discussed later on. The European markets tend to move very closely in tandem with the United States market, but Asian markets, particularly those in the Far East, often rise and fall at different times than ours.

- **International small companies.** Foreign small companies, like domestic ones, are more speculative than larger companies, but do have above-average rates of return and provide geographic as well as industry diversification. Foreign stocks, as a group, tend to perform better than domestic issues during periods that the U.S. dollar is losing value compared to foreign currencies, so, in a sense, investments made in overseas markets represent a hedge against weakness in our currency.

Using Mutual Funds to Represent Diversified Sectors

The mutual fund industry provides numerous vehicles that represent the sectors listed previously. For example, Fidelity Real Estate Investors Class (Symbol, FRESX), Fidelity Select Food and Agriculture (FDFAX), Fidelity Select Insurance (FSPCX), Franklin Utilities (FSPTX) and Vanguard Energy/Inv (VGENX), Vanguard Health Care (VGHCX), and AIM Leisure/Inv (FLISX) are fine funds that represent their market sectors well.

Rosters of mutual funds are available from all major mutual fund management companies. Further information relating to mutual funds may be secured from Morningstar publications.

Exchange traded funds (ETFs), to be discussed later, also provide very ready means of placing investments in varied and specific industry sectors.

The diversified portfolio is again by no means the only form of diversification that investors may create. For example, income-oriented mutual funds or actual bonds may be included in the blend to reduce risk and to provide at least some predictable income flow.

The main point is to create and to maintain well-diversified portfolios. We imagine that readers should have the point by now.

A Basic Strategy

In chapters to come, you will learn ways to identify sectors that are leading in strength and a relatively simple way to track changes in leadership, coupled with a strategy of regularly rotating your portfolio so that the largest portion of your assets are invested in the strongest areas.

One approach that you may want to take for a portion of your portfolio is to place perhaps 10–15% of your stock-related positions in a diversified portfolio represented by the sectors listed previously— perhaps 1/8 of the assets so dedicated for each sector.

This would generally be maintained as a buy and hold area of your portfolio, with periodic rebalancing, as discussed later in the chapter. We believe that there is a strong likelihood that over the years, the blend shown will perform quite well with reduced risk compared to more concentrated portfolio blends.

Active Diversification Strategies— To Maintain the Balance

As specific market sectors ebb and flow in their strength relative to each other, the composition of your portfolio diversification is likely to become skewed so that investments in recently leading sectors become disproportionately large in relationship to the whole of your investment portfolio. Although the temptation to allow stronger groups to be overweighted in portfolio compared to weaker groups is considerable—as well as often a good strategy—the over-weighting of leading market sectors can be carried so far as to defeat the benefits of diversification.

Case History

For example, let's suppose that at the start of 1970 (which marked the end of a technology boom from an earlier generation), two investors decided that they liked technology stocks but recognized the inherent risks involved. As a result, each resolved to place half of his assets in a safe bond mutual fund and the other half in a technology fund.

Investor A was the more obsessive of the two and so, at the end of every quarter, he checked his portfolio. If the balance of assets in the technology fund and bond fund had deviated from the precise 50/50 mix with which he had started, he would sell some of one holding and buy some of the other in order to restore the desired 50/50 balance. For example, if technology had performed better than bonds during a quarter, then by the end of the quarter, more than half his invested assets would be in technology, less than half in bonds. Therefore, in order to restore the original 50/50 allocation between technology funds and bonds, he would have to sell off some of his technology fund holdings and use the proceeds to buy some additional bonds. This process is referred to as "rebalancing."

Investor B did not want to expend the effort and, moreover, pre-ferred to ride with the "hot" area of his portfolio, so he just let his original investments in technology and bonds rise and fall as they might.

Figure 2.1 shows how the performance of these two investors evolved between 1970–2007, assuming that their investments per-formed consistently with average funds in these two sectors: technology and bond funds.

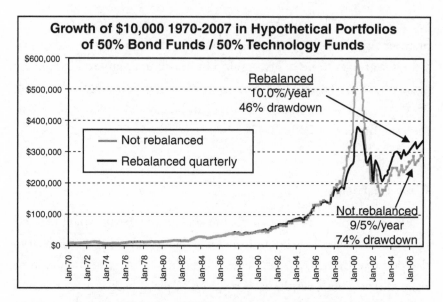

Figure 2.1 The long-term benefits of quarterly rebalancing. In the long run, the portfolio that was rebalanced to keep its segments equal performed better than the portfolio that was allowed to become highly skewed.

As you can see, the investor who rebalanced his portfolio regularly kept removing profits from the table as he cashed in profits from technology and placed them into bond funds. Investor A did incur losses during the bear market, but not to the extent of Investor B, who was clearly ahead as year 2000 started, but ended behind Investor A as late as 2006.

Drawbacks to Rebalancing

Rebalancing at regular intervals does have its drawbacks. It does create transaction expenses and extra taxable transactions as profits are taken. And it may, potentially, remove capital from stronger positions before they have run their course.

A Compromise Solution That Provides the Best of Both Worlds

You will learn in subsequent chapters the benefits of investing in the best-performing market areas rather than simply in all areas equally. At the same time, diversification very definitely has its benefits. The solution to the conflict? Compromise.

In this case, you might want to start equally but to allow a certain amount of deviation from the balance to take place before rebalancing. For example, if you were to hold a portfolio consisting of 50% of bonds and 50% of technology stocks, you might not begin to sell off technology until it became 60% of the portfolio (10% above its original 50% balance level) and bonds declined to 40% of the mix. You would set a 60% maximum for each segment and a 40% minimum.

Suppose you have an eight segment multi-sector portfolio—each sector starting with 12½% of initial assets. Let's suppose that the international sector was very strong over the years, with the value of its assets rising to 22½% of the whole. If you had planned to allow for a 10% deviation from the average, you would then sell off assets from that area if and when its value exceeded 22½% of the whole, placing the proceeds, perhaps, into a sector whose values had fallen far below its original 12½% allocation.

This procedure, rebalancing when segments of your portfolio had become extremely profitable compared to the average segment, will automatically cause you to "sell into strength" rather than buy into strength (which the public tends to do) and to "buy into weakness," generally a pretty good idea as well.

Just to restate, sell positions whose proportion of your portfolio mix has climbed to above 10% more than its asset allocation and buy positions whose asset value has declined by 10% from its asset percentage allocation.

One More Example

You initiate a three-segment diversified portfolio consisting of 33⅓% Standard & Poor's 500 Index, 33⅓% bonds, and 33⅓% international holdings—the total, 100% of assets. In due course, the internationals perform well so that their value rises to 45% of your entire portfolio. Bonds, in the meantime, decline to 21% of the value of your total portfolio. The Standard & Poor's 500 Index holding, in the interim, has risen to 34% of the total portfolio value (45% + 21% +34% = 100%). We are allowing a 10% deviation from the average share (33⅓% + 10% = 43⅓%).

You might reduce your international position from 45% to 43⅓% of portfolio, 10% above its starting share of 33⅓% of assets. The proceeds from your sale would be placed into the bond segment, increasing its value at the time from 21% to 22⅔%% of portfolio, still a little underweighted (more than 10% below its fair share of 33⅓%) but close enough.

Summing Up

You considered two scenarios and alternative approaches to portfolio rebalancing combined with the maintenance of diversification. Other variations are viable, of course, but they should lie within the frameworks noted.

Referring to Historical Drawdowns to Measure Risk

Investor psychology tends to fluctuate with market cycles. Following a bear market of the extent of the 2000–2002 bear market (or the bear markets of 1969–1970, 1973–1974), investors tend to be highly fixated on market risk. The most money tends to flow into the stock market following long periods of market rise, not early in the advance.

As bullish advances proceed along, investors tend to become most fixated on potential profits, the sense of risk diminishing with each month of rising stock prices until the world of investment becomes, in effect, a universe of speculation.

It goes without saying—at least, hopefully, among this book's readers—that risk control is probably at least as and probably more essential for profitable investing than attention to profit potential.

How risky can risk be? Well, it should also go without saying that if an investment has incurred a certain amount of loss in the past, that amount of loss represents—**at a minimum**—the risk potential in the future. If you want to assess the potential risk of a stock, of a mutual fund, or of the stock market as a whole, you may do so by checking out that investment vehicle's past performance to see what has been the worst loss that has occurred in the past, using at least three or four decades of history for review.

For example, you might examine Figure 2.2, the history of Microsoft (MSFT) between 1996–2007. Figure 2.2 identifies the largest percentage decline in MSFT during this period, which was a 63.3% loss sustained between 12/27/1999 and 12/20/2000. The largest loss from the peak value of an investment to its subsequent low point is called the *drawdown*. Drawdown is a measure of investment risk: The worse the historical drawdowns, the riskier the investment.

The Perils of Minimizing Risk

As Microsoft soared in price from 1996 to late 1999, who would have thought that the stock was capable of declining from its peak by more than 63% in less than one year?

However, it did.

The Midcap SPDR Exchange Traded Fund—Another Example

Figure 2.3 illustrates another example of drawdown (risk): the Midcap SPDR (symbol MDY).

Figure 2.2 The maximum drawdown of an investment is the greatest percentage decline from a peak price to its subsequent low price, prior to a recovery to a new peak. As of mid-2007, the largest drawdown seen by Microsoft had been 63.3%.

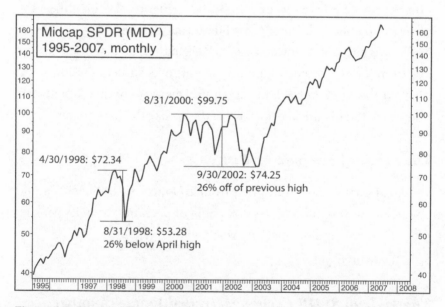

Figure 2.3 The monthly drawdowns of the Midcap SPDR 1995–2007. The 26% decline in the Midcap SPDR in 1998 provided warning of the risk involved in this index. The 1998 decline, as matters turned out, was replicated between 2002 and 2003.

The histories of Microsoft and of the Midcap SPDR (MDY) illustrate the risks that can manifest themselves even in connection with investments that are in strong long-term uptrends. The Midcap SPDRs have overcome all drawdowns to rise to new high levels during 2004; Microsoft has not yet recovered to its 1999 highs. Once again, in evaluating risk, do take your study period back at least two and preferably three decades.

Drawdowns Are Often Worse Than You Think

The chart of the MDY (see Figure 2.3) reflects monthly closes. The high areas are based on end-of-month prices, as are the low areas. Actually, this form of chart minimizes the extent of drawdown or losses seen since it would be rare for either the actual high price or the actual low price to be recorded at the last day of each month. Highs and/or lows are more likely to take place mid-month.

Figure 2.4 illustrates this point.

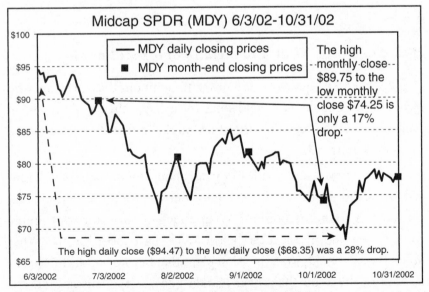

Figure 2.4 Differences between drawdowns calculated on a daily and monthly basis. The highest drawdown shown based on monthly closings is only 17%. However, if daily closing prices are employed, we can see that the actual maximum drawdown was actually 28%.

As you can see, the decline from the actual peak reading, June 3, 2002, and the lowest daily reading, early October 2002, was 28%. Based on monthly close data, however, the maximum drawdown was only 17%.

Mentally Making the Correction

If you are studying monthly data, just mentally add about 10% to the shown drawdowns to estimate intra-month or daily-based drawdowns.

It may be difficult to secure daily mutual fund pricing data, but you can secure a pretty good estimate of a fund's risk simply by reviewing yearly price changes, which are readily available from fund families or from Morningstar. Compare yearly returns of funds with major market indices such as the Standard & Poor's 500 Index and/or with mutual funds of similar investment objectives to see how risk and reward relationships have been over the years.

Risk Control Is Vital, Financially and Emotionally

Stock market apologists are prone to point out that investors who have simply bought and held long term have almost always been bailed out in the long run—the stock market, after all, has been in a long-term up trend.

This is all well and good. But what about the investor who has to start to withdraw capital for living expenses during the periods that the stock market hits bottom? What about the investor who simply cannot bear more risk after heavy losses have been taken? What about the major corporate pension plans that became underfunded as a result of the 2000–2002 bear market because the trustees did not factor risks fully into their projections?

You are learning some good strategies to control risk. Employ them.

Bond-Stock Balanced Portfolios

As you may recall, in Chapter 1 we discussed portfolios structured as blends of bonds and stocks, concluding that the best balances between these two classes of investment lie in the area of 60% stocks–40% bonds, or even 50% each, or even 40% stocks–60% bonds. In the past, long-term profits have been only slightly reduced while risks have been decreased significantly.

At this time, bonds are not yielding as much as in previous decades, so stocks have been showing higher than normal outperformance compared to bond investments in recent years. These relationships may or may not continue in the years to come.

The Two Major Vehicles for Diversified Investment: Mutual Funds and Exchange Traded Funds

Mutual funds—join the other guys in trusting the manager … time tested, true enough, but you do give up something in the way of flexibility and expenses

Mutual funds are popular, well known, and advertise freely and frequently to secure shareholders. Certain mutual fund families of funds—such as Fidelity, Vanguard, T. Rowe Price, and Dreyfus—are household names, closely followed by millions of investors as well as the press.

Still, despite their popularity, there are definite advantages and disadvantages to investing in mutual funds that, we believe, are worth reviewing.

Pooled Capital—Professional Management

Mutual funds are vehicles that allow investors to pool their money, which is turned over to investment professionals to manage for them. In theory—if definitely not necessarily in practice—professional managers will have the ability to produce investment results that are superior to what a smaller investor might accomplish on his own with random investment selection.

The management of the mutual fund invests the assets entrusted to it and selects investments consistent with the investment objectives of the fund (which are set forth in each mutual fund's prospectus). Most available mutual funds hold individual stocks, bonds, or both, sometimes domestic issues, sometimes foreign issues, sometimes a blend.

Benefits of Mutual Funds

The mutual fund structure allows individual investors with relatively small amounts of capital to own (indirectly) highly diversified portfolios without having to track and/or pay separate commissions for each holding. In general, smaller investors do save on commission costs by purchasing mutual funds rather than a portfolio of the separate holdings of mutual funds.

Although the majority of mutual funds do not particularly outperform the average market stock, some portfolio managers do have outstanding performance records and have added value in excess of management fees charged to investors.[1]

The majority of mutual funds allow investors to open and/or add capital to their holdings or to remove capital from their holdings without sales charges. These are referred to as "no-load" funds. *We do not recommend the purchase of mutual funds for which you have to pay commissions, either at the time of the transaction (front-load) or at the time of redemption (back-end load). There are simply too many fine funds available that are commission free.*

Buying and Selling Mutual Funds

After the close of trading each day (generally 4 p.m. eastern time), mutual funds tally and report the share value of its portfolio—the total value of all its holdings less owed expenses of the fund divided by the number of shares outstanding. The value per share thus calculated is referred to as the "net asset value." If you buy shares during the day, your cost per share will be the next net asset value calculated after you place your order. If you sell, your sales price will be the next asset value calculated after you place your order. For example, if you place your order at mid-day, you will transact at the price calculated immediately following the close of trading that day. If you place your order after the market close, the transaction will take place at the closing price of the next trading day.

The ability to buy additional shares or to redeem at no expense can be valuable and in past years was employed by active investors who desired to trade mutual funds short term. This freedom to trade frequently is no longer available (something of a disadvantage to mutual funds). The ability to trade only at days' end is also potentially something of a disadvantage to mutual fund investors, but does serve to reduce impulsive trading.

Taken all in all, "buy" and "sell" procedures for mutual funds are rather favorable for investors, if not necessarily ideal. Remember: The main things to avoid are extra expenses connected with many mutual funds, such as high management expenses, buying and selling commissions, and/or particularly odious redemption restrictions.

You Get an Immediate Portfolio

When you buy shares of most mutual funds, you do not buy existing shares from someone else. Rather, your money goes into the fund that, in turn, creates new shares for you, which immediately provides you with proportional ownership of all the stocks and bonds that the fund already owned at the time it received your investment. The type of mutual fund that can create as many shares as needed to accommodate new investments is referred to as an open-end fund. Open-end funds are the most popular of mutual funds, but there is a category of mutual funds referred to as closed-end funds that have their own stipulations, benefits, and disadvantages.[2]

The Downside—Nothing Is for Nothing

There are expenses involved with investments in mutual fund shares, which do reduce their benefits. First, fund managers and management companies have to be paid. The fund is liable for expenses for filings, auditing, paperwork, mailings, and SEC compliance, which are passed along to shareholders. These and other expenses are passed along to shareholders as the "expense ratio" of the fund.

The expense ratio is the fraction of the fund's assets consumed each year for the expenses listed previously. For most equity funds, expense ratios average approximately 1% per year. Some fund families such as Vanguard are particularly inexpensive in this regard. Other funds, usually those that trade frequently, have expense ratios in excess of 2% per year. Expense ratios represent expenses that reduce shareholder profit and place the fund at a disadvantage when its performance is compared with market indices, which have no expenses. Taken all in all, the lower the expense ratios, the better.[3]

Scurvy Selling Practices of Mutual Funds and How You Can Beat Them

Banks, financial planners, and brokerage houses often steer customers to load funds because as selling agents, they receive a good portion of your commission charges. These should be avoided. If you invest $100 into a mutual fund, you want all of that $100 to go into your investment—not $95, after the brokerage takes its share.

A sneakier policy involves the steering of customers to "Class B shares," shares for which you do not pay a front-end commission (load). Instead, you are charged back-end redemption commissions of up to 6% if you redeem within a year, such commissions reduced year by year until usually, after six years of ownership, you are finally liberated. Class B shares generally have higher expense ratios than other shares, because they pay to the sales agency annual payouts, usually around 0.75% per year, for bringing in the business. So the customer ends up "locked" into what may be a poorly performing fund by the expense of selling out, and also in a vehicle with higher expense ratios than anyone should have to pay.

Figure 2.5 illustrates the differential in net performance between Class A shares of Pimco Total Return and Class B shares of the same fund. Both hold the same assets. Class B shareholders simply have payout costs to salespeople deducted from their assets.

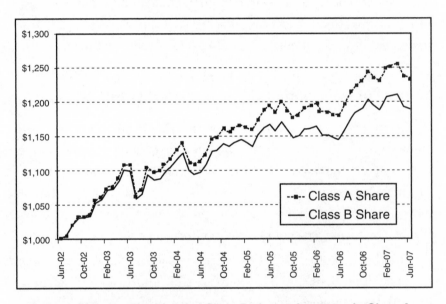

Figure 2.5 The disadvantages of Class B shares. Investors in Class A shares of Pimco Total Return secure increasingly superior returns over the years than investors in Class B shares.

We think you get the idea by now. If your broker or advisor tries to steer you to Class B shares, let him or her know that you know the score and consider taking your business elsewhere.

How to Beat the System

Many discount brokerage firms such as Schwab or T.D. Ameritrade provide to customers the ability to **purchase load mutual funds at no front-end loads at all.** You pay only a generally moderate transaction cost to the brokerage. For example, although Pimco Total Return charges up to 3.75% for Class A shares, you could purchase shares at T.D. Ameritrade at no mutual fund commission whatsoever, just a relatively small transaction fee.

Summing Up

Popular open-end mutual funds provide many opportunities for creative portfolio management. Investors should, however, remain cognizant of investment expenses and of the past performance, expense ratios, and investment objectives of funds in which they invest.

Sources of Information Regarding Mutual Funds

Morningstar Funds 500 (Wiley Publishers) contains a large amount of information regarding 500 diversified mutual funds, including all the areas mentioned previously and more. Caveat! Morningstar assigns performance ***** star ratings to funds that have no particular value insofar as predicting future performance. Visit www.morningstar.com for more information.

Another site to visit is www.finance.yahoo.com. Check under "Mutual Fund Screener" for many areas of information. The site is free. At www.moneycentral.msn.com, click on "fundresearch" to find numerous performance and other screens regarding mutual funds. Both sites provide free charts of mutual funds.

Exchange Traded Funds (ETFs)— The New Kid on the Block

For many, many years, mutual funds held a monopoly as the investment vehicle of choice for smaller investors who wanted a simple means of investing with the assistance of professional management teams. The popularity of mutual funds remained essentially intact, even though the majority of mutual funds did not actually outperform unmanaged market indices such as the Standard & Poor's 500 Index, with the expenses of mutual funds putting them under a handicap that their management firms could not generally overcome.

Enter the SPDRs

In recent years, a new form of mutual fund has come to the fore—a form of fund with many advantages (and some disadvantages) compared to the traditional mutual fund. This form is called "the exchange traded fund" or "ETF." The initial fund of the type, the SPDRs (Standard & Poor's 500 Depository Receipts), was introduced in the early 1990s, since which time this particular ETF and its descendents have become very popular. Figure 2.6 shows the rapid growth in the number of available ETFs and the total assets invested in ETFs from 2002 through early 2007.

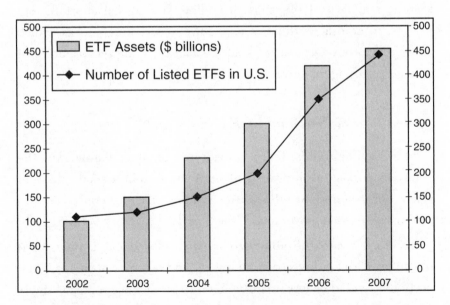

Figure 2.6 Growth in the number of ETFs and in ETF assets, 2002–2007 (through 3/31/2007).

ETFs are created by various organizations (such as mutual fund families, banks, and other financial institutions) that create and package stock and/or bond portfolios representing certain market indices and sectors into units that are sold on the stock market exchanges as shares of ETF securities. ETFs are generally traded on the open market between buyers and sellers (unlike mutual funds, which are traded between shareholders and the management company). If there are more buyers than ETFs available for sale, the firm responsible for maintaining an orderly trading environment (called a specialist) can simply create more units by buying and packaging stocks that the ETF represents. If there are more sellers of ETFs than there are buyers, the specialist firm can purchase the surplus and then liquidate the units by selling the individual shares that comprise the ETF.

If this seems complicated, just keep in mind that ETFs are mutual funds that you can buy and sell during the day, without trading limits but with bid-ask spreads and transaction costs. ETFs represent a plethora of popular domestic and international markets, industry sectors, and special offerings that allow you to sell short market indices, to hold a portfolio of above average yielding stocks, which allow you to buy technology, health, small caps, large caps, and just about everything in between.

Special Perks Provided by ETFS

Like mutual funds, ETFS provide to potential shareholders the ability to package well-diversified portfolios within a single share of stock. For example, SPDRS (ticker symbol SPY) are constructed to replicate the price movement of the Standard & Poor's 500 Index.

ETFs provide the ability to create well-balanced, diversified portfolios with holdings of just a few individual types of shares. Such portfolios tend to be less volatile and more predictable than just single company holdings in representing market sectors.

The sponsors of ETFS make their money from expense ratios that they charge to shareholders for packaging and managing the distribution of ETFs. Such expense ratios are generally well below the costs charged to shareholders by regular mutual fund companies. Note: ETFs do not represent managed portfolios. Rather, like index mutual funds, their composition is designed to reflect either well-known stock market indices (such as the Dow Jones Industrial Average or the Nasdaq Composite) or certain pre-designed investment styles (for example, high-dividend stock ETFs). Once the portfolios are set, that is the mix represented by a particular ETF. One of the reasons why ETFs have lower expenses than mutual funds is that ETFs do not bear the expense of hiring a professional manager.

There are often more favorable tax consequences associated with ETF than with mutual funds. If you buy shares of a mutual fund and the company declares a capital gain dividend, you may well be subject to income taxes on that dividend, even though the fund price drops by the amount of payout, so in the end you have not really made a profit. ETFs are much less subject to taxes on such phantom profits.

Nothing's for Nothing

When you trade mutual funds, you may not know what price you will be paying until after the close of the market that day, but you do know that you will be paying one price for all the shares you want to buy, that you will be receiving one price for all the shares you want to sell, and that all shareholders trading that day will get the same price.

ETFs trade like stocks and bonds. There are "bid prices" (the price at which buyers are willing to buy) and "asked prices" (prices asked by sellers). If you buy at the "asked" and sell at the "bid," the spread (asked price minus bid price) represents a loss that has to be made up. Regular mutual funds have no spreads.

And, of course, there are generally commissions to be paid to the brokerage, unless you trade via a brokerage house that charges a "wrap fee," a generally annual fee that you pay regardless of how many trades you make.

ETFs, again, provide no active management—a plus or a minus depending upon your attitude regarding mutual fund managers.

CAVEAT: Although ETFs are generally advertised as representing a stock market area, in fact sponsors often employ just a few issues to represent a broader market sector or index, which does create situations in which ETFs do not exactly track their nominal benchmark.

Finally, ETFs have become truly popular only in recent years. All the plethora of problems that can develop may not, as yet, have been experienced.

All caveats aside, ETFs do provide investors with a useful arena for the ready creation of portfolios marked by full diversification, with emphasis on the sector(s) of your choice, and ready liquidity.

Examples of ETFs

Income ETFs
- ***iShares Lehman TIPS Bond Fund (TIP).** Invests in treasury inflation-protected securities (discussed further in Chapter 7, "Special Bond Market Investment Oportunities").

Global Investment
- **Vanguard Emerging Markets Vipers (VWO).** Emerging market equity investments.

Domestic Market Indices

- **Diamond Series Trust I (DIA).** Designed to replicate the movement of the Dow Industrials.
- **SPDR 500 (SPY).** Designed to replicate the movement of the Standard & Poor's 500 Index.
- **IShares Russell 2000 Value (IWN).** Replicates the small capitalization value index.

Specific Overseas Countries

• **iShares MSCI Brazil Index (EWZ).* Reflects the Brazilian stock market.

We will be showing you a number of useful strategies by which you can profitably invest in diversified portfolios involving these and other vehicles.

Further Information

There are numerous websites that provide information regarding ETFs.

You can search the Internet for "exchange traded funds" or "ETFs."

One of our long-standing favorite websites in this regard is www.etfconnect.com, a site that also provides good information regarding "closed-end" mutual funds, special types of mutual funds that have advantages and disadvantages of their own. At www.price-data.com, you can secure current prices and symbols of listed ETFs.[4]

3

Prelude to Long-Term Wealth—
Introduction to the Stock Market

*"I don't know what the seven wonders of the world are, but
I do know the eighth: compound interest."*

—Baron Rothschild[1]

Stocks have provided a ticket to wealth for long-term investors for generations. In fact, between 1926–2006, the value of a stock market investment has returned more than 10%/year, outpacing inflation by 7% annually, on average. Although real estate has been an excellent investment as well, stocks have enjoyed a stronger long-term growth rate historically. Figure 3.1 shows the growth of $1,000 from 1921–2006 in large U.S. company stocks including dividends compared to the growth of home prices and inflation during the same period. (Of course, stock market performance in any given year is likely to deviate far from that average, for better or worse.)

However, the trip from where you are financially to where you would like to be can be dangerous without a knowledgeable guide. And who better to guide you than yourself?

This chapter describes several specific areas of the stock market that you will learn how to exploit for greater gains in Chapter 4, "Nothing Succeeds Like Success." Although stocks usually rise and fall as a group, different clusters of companies (called *investment styles*) have tended to be stronger than others, often for years at a time. In Chapter 4, you will learn how to pick the stronger investment styles by evaluating their performances every three months. The result has been a significant improvement in performance from the expenditure of a very modest amount of effort.

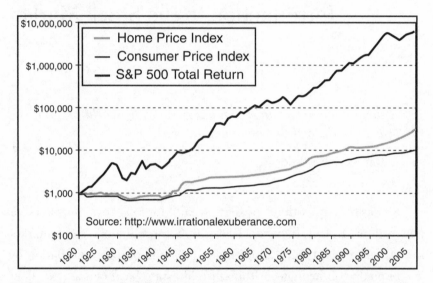

Figure 3.1 Growth of $1,000 in U.S. stocks, housing, and inflation from 1921–2006. (Source: www.irrationalexuberance.com)

Broad Portfolios at Bargain Rates—Index Funds

An *index* is a basket of stocks selected by an index sponsor to represent a particular area of the stock market. Indexes can be very broad (such as the Morgan Stanley All Country World Index, which attempts to reflect the overall behavior of all the world's stock markets) or very narrow (such as the Standard and Poor's Homebuilding Index,[2] which consists of 22 stocks in American companies that build houses).

Originally, indexes were designed to provide a shortcut for investors who wanted a sense of how the stock market was doing. The oldest indexes still in use are the Dow Jones Industrial Average and the Dow Jones Transportation Average, which were launched in 1896.

Other indexes developed to serve a similar function include the S&P 500 Index (representing large U.S. companies) and the Russell 2000 Index (representing small U.S. companies).

The baskets of stocks that comprise today's most widely-used indexes are generally re-evaluated once every year, although some index providers adjust the basket of stocks in their indexes as frequently as every three months or less than once a year (Dow Jones Industrial Average). Their goal is to represent the performance of a particular investment area rather than to beat it, so index providers do not generally have to research the companies in their indexes in as much depth as many investment managers might want to. In fact, a number of indexes simply average the behavior of all stocks available on U.S. exchanges (for example, Dow Jones Wilshire 5000) or just the largest 3000 stocks (Russell 3000 Index), requiring no research at all.

Index funds are mutual funds whose portfolios are designed to mirror the action of market indexes. The first index funds tracked pre-existing indexes, such as the S&P 500, with long pedigrees. However, since the late 1990s, many indexes have been developed with the express purpose of being used as the basis for an investment product rather than for the purpose of providing an overview of part of the stock market. It is not clear whether investments designed to follow these newer indexes will provide the demonstrated benefits (described later in the chapter) of investments that track traditional indexes.

Compared to the number of transactions in the average actively managed mutual fund, the composition of most market indexes changes relatively little from one year to the next. As a result, index fund portfolios require relatively few transactions and little or no research to maintain, so investments that track stock market indexes generally have lower internal expenses than mutual funds with active managers. Index funds have received a lot of favorable press over the years because their performance has been better than that of most regular mutual funds.

Index funds offered by Vanguard or Fidelity have very low expenses, and they offer individuals most of the same advantages of more expensive mutual funds. You can add or redeem from your investment without cost, and you can avail yourself of shareholder services including tax reporting. Investors looking for the lowest cost option for putting their money to work in the stock market, and who want to make frequent small additions to their accounts (such as through payroll deductions) should utilize low-cost index funds such as those that track the S&P 500 Index.[3]

There are only two disadvantages of index mutual funds. First, most limit the frequency with which you can sell and repurchase shares. For example, you cannot sell shares of the Vanguard S&P 500 Index Fund and then re-enter the same fund a week or a month later because as a matter of policy, Vanguard funds prohibit repurchasing shares in their equity funds within 60 days of a redemption.[4] Some other Vanguard funds impose minimum one-year holding periods. As you will see in later chapters, such restrictions can hamper your ability to get the highest possible returns and minimize investment risk. Second, there are many areas of the market for which few or no index funds are available. Exchange-traded funds (ETFs) solve both of these problems, which is why we recommend ETFs to implement the strategies in Chapters 4 and 5.

The Types of Mutual Fund and ETF Portfolios You Should Invest in

If you want to set up a permanent investment portfolio—funds that you can buy and leave alone—here are the five basic items that every one of you should have:

- Large U.S. company stocks
- Small U.S. company value stocks
- Stocks in companies that own and manage real estate (called real estate investment trusts, or REITs)
- Bond funds (floating rate and low-expense investment grade bond funds)
- International funds (see Chapter 5, "Worldwide Opportunity")

Large and small company U.S. stocks, real estate investment trusts (REITs), and the notion of a value stock are all explained later in this chapter. International stocks are covered in more detail in Chapter 5, and the different types of bond funds are discussed in Chapter 6, "Bonds—An Investment for All Seasons," Chapter 7, "Special Bond Market Investment Opportunities," and Chapter 8, "Treasure in the Junkyard—How to Tame High Yield Bonds."

As an illustration of how you can use this list, Table 3.1 contains a portfolio of mutual funds that you could buy once at a discount brokerage mutual fund platform and then ignore, except for occasional rebalancing. In those areas where index funds have performed better than the majority of actively managed mutual funds, we have recommended index funds from Vanguard. Otherwise, we have recommended actively managed alternatives that have been superior (compared to most mutual funds with similar objectives) in terms of the historical balance between their rewards and risk. In the case of the Oppenheimer Floating Rate Fund, class A, purchase these shares only if you can do so without paying a sales commission, as is possible at T.D. Ameritrade, for example. (This type of fund is discussed in more detail in Chapter 7.)

TABLE 3.1 Representative Portfolio of Mutual Funds for Long-Term Growth

Mutual Fund	Ticker Symbol	Objective	Percent of Portfolio
Vanguard 500 Index Fund	VFINX	Large U.S. company stocks	25%
Vanguard Small-Cap Value Index Fund	VISVX	Small U.S. company value stocks	15%
Fidelity Real Estate Investment Portfolio	FRESX	REITs	15%
Vanguard Intermediate-Term Bond Market Index	VBIIX	Intermediate-term U.S. investment-grade bonds	13%
Oppenheimer Senior Floating Rate A	XOSAX	Floating-rate bank loans	12%
Vanguard Total International Stock Market Index	VGTSX	Non-U.S. stock markets (developed and emerging)	20%

As a general principle, we do not recommend sticking with a single portfolio through all market conditions, because there are different opportunities in the market at different times, and taking advantage of them with a more active approach has added to returns and helped reduce risk. Nonetheless, if you decide that you do want to maintain a consistent portfolio at all times, the roster of funds in Table 3.1 could well put you ahead of most investors if past patterns repeat themselves in the future (which is never guaranteed, unfortunately).

Whales Versus Minnows: Large and Small Company Stocks

Back in the old days (1970s and before), the most popular way to rank companies was embodied by the Fortune 500 list, which is based on the volume of sales a company made. However, the technology bubble rendered obsolete the quaint notion that a company's size should be measured by how much it sells (or by how many people it employs). Today, company size is all about the value of a company's stock: The greater the value of a company's shares, the larger its weight in calculating most market indexes.

The value of a company is the number of total shares that exist times the current share price. For example, if a company has a billion shares outstanding and the current share price is $20/share, then the value of the company's stock, called the market capitalization, is $20 billion (1 billion shares × $20/share).[5] As a practical matter, if you had $20 billion, you could not buy all the shares of this company because in attempting to do so, you would likely drive up the price of the stock.

Companies whose shares are worth over $10 billion total are called *large-cap* companies. Companies whose shares are worth $2 billion or less in total are called *small-cap* companies. Companies whose market capitalizations lie within the $2–$10 billion range are called *midcap* companies. These distinctions are important because simply knowing the size of the companies in different portfolios can tell you which of them are likely to be favored in the current economic environment. We will present a powerful method of selecting the preferred grouping of stocks (small versus large companies) in Chapter 4.

The business climate is not constant. At some times, there are reasons for much confidence: The economy is growing, interest rates are low, and companies as a whole enjoy pricing power. Small companies are particularly able to capitalize on this type of environment to grow. As a result, during favorable economic climates, small company stocks are likely to outperform large company stocks.

Conversely, during periods of poor business confidence, slowing growth, inability to pass cost increases to customers, or difficulty getting loans, small companies face disproportionate challenges and their stocks are likely to lag behind large company stocks. Overall, small companies are riskier than large ones. They have a greater likelihood of failing, and are subject to greater risk exposure to individual customers or suppliers of importance.

Not only are small companies inherently riskier than large ones, but because they generally have fewer shares outstanding, their stocks are more difficult (and costly) to trade than large-cap stocks. It is sometimes harder to find a willing buyer or seller of shares in a small company at any given price, particularly for a large number of shares. This gives individual investors an advantage over large institutions in the small-cap arena. You can move your own capital in or out of small-cap equity investments whenever you judge such a move to be advantageous without moving the market against you. A large pension fund trying to do the same thing may find it is like trying to steer an aircraft carrier in a confined area.

From your perspective as an investor, the important thing about small-cap stocks is that over the long term, they have returned more than large-cap stocks. Table 3.2 shows the relative gains and risks in small-, mid-, and large-cap stocks from 1926–2004.[6] If you are curious as to whether a particular company is classified as small, mid, or large cap, you can look up its stock in Yahoo Finance or MSN Money. On the quote page for each stock is its total market capitalization. (The precise URLs for these websites are listed in the Appendix "Internet Resources for Investors.")

TABLE 3.2 Historical Returns and Relative Risk Levels from Small, Medium, and Large Company Stocks, 1926–2004

Market Capitalization	Compounded Annual Total Return	Relative Risk[7]
Largest stocks (top 10% of stocks by market cap)	9.6%	1.0
Middle range (stocks in 30th–50th percentile by market cap)	11.4%	1.3
Smaller companies (stocks in the 60th–80th percentile by market cap)	11.8%	1.5

The information in Table 3.2 raises the question of whether small caps always do better, or whether it is worth trying to identify those periods when small caps are likely to outperform large caps and invest in small caps only during those periods. Although we mentioned earlier that small-cap value stocks (a subset of the small-cap stock universe whose performance appears in Table 3.2) should be part of a permanent investment portfolio for those of you who do not want to place any transactions, we strongly recommend that you take a more opportunistic approach, investing in small-cap stocks only when the market environment appears favorable for that area. The data in Figure 3.2 show you why: Small-cap stocks have gone for many years at a time without beating large caps. In fact, it is only in the past 32 years (1975–2006) out of 81 that small caps have outperformed large caps, and during those 32 years, small caps were stronger only about half the time (1975–1983, 1999–2006).

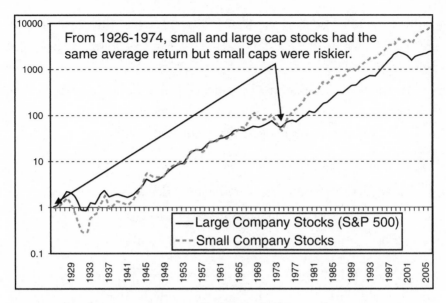

Figure 3.2 Long-term growth of $1 (1926–2006) in large-cap and small-cap stocks.

Bargain Hunting or Headline Chasing: Value Versus Growth

The value versus growth dichotomy could be stated as stocks that are either inexpensive based on where the company stands now (value), or worth paying more than average to buy now for their assets and income in return for above-average future prospects (growth). There is no universal agreement on a definition of growth or value. Some criteria frequently used to identify stocks as value stocks include the following:

- Above-average dividend yield
- Above-average profits (relative to share value)
- Above-average sales (relative to share value)
- Above-average underlying assets (relative to share value)

Although not every stock can be considered cheaper than average based on every one of these measurements of relative value, as a practical matter there is significant overlap: Stocks that have above-average dividend yields also tend to have above-average profitability, and so on.

Even though value stocks can be in any number of different industries, as a group they have tended to behave similarly in several respects compared to the overall stock market, as follows:

1. Lower volatility.

2. Smaller losses during overall market declines.

3. Smaller gains during overall market advances.

4. Dividends represent a larger share of total return.

Although historically, value stocks have risen more slowly than the overall market during bull market periods, during the market advance of 2004–2006, value stocks were actually stronger than the overall market. One of the reasons why value stocks have been so strong is that large oil companies, utilities, and large financial services companies tend to be disproportionately represented among the ranks of value stocks, and these industries have been especially fortunate in the past few years (2003–2006).

Not Every Bargain Is Worth Buying

Although value stocks as a group have beaten the market over the long term, not every stock that appears cheap has ended up being a good investment. Eastman Kodak (EK) is an example. At the start of 2003, EK was paying dividends of $1.80/share on a share price of $35 (dividend yield of 5.1%), much more generous than the S&P 500 Index yield of 2.2% at that time. EK earned $2.89/share in 2002, which was an above-average profit level relative to the share price. In the absence of a negative outlook for the underlying business, EK appeared to be an excellent buy.

However, the dividend yield was if anything unfairly low in retrospect: Investors who bought at $35/share at the start of 2003 saw EK cut its dividend from $1.80 to $0.50/share that year. Annual earnings per share fell from $2.89/share in 2002 to $1.75/share in 2003, and the share price itself fell from $35.04 to $25.67—a total return loss of 23% in a year when the S&P 500 Index returned over 28%.

On the other hand, General Motors (GM) started out in 2006 with a 10% dividend yield that was widely viewed as unsustainably high. GM did in fact cut its dividend in half during 2006, but nonetheless the stock far outperformed the overall market.

This brings us to growth stocks. Unlike value stocks, which are often "boring," the stories behind growth stocks can be very appealing. When you buy growth stocks, you are betting that company's future successes will measure up to expectations. Of course, the bandwagon for hot stocks is crowded, so you have to pay more for your ticket to ride.

Table 3.3 shows that the long-term profitability (from 1969–2004) of value stocks has been greater than that of growth stocks through multiple cycles of up and down markets. Table 3.3 also shows that value stocks as a group were safer than growth stocks—a violation of the expected pattern that in order to earn a greater return, an investor must bear greater risk. Stated another way, in theory there is not supposed to be any way to reduce risk without reducing return (except by diversification), yet value investing seems to have offered one.

TABLE 3.3 Compounded Annual Gains and Relative Risks for Value and Growth Stocks[8]

Investment Style	Compounded Annual Total Return	Relative Risk[9]
Large-Cap Value	11.0%	0.9
Large-Cap Growth	9.3%	1.1
Small-Cap Value	15.4%	1.2
Small-Cap Growth	9.3%	1.4

Therefore, if you have to choose only one type of strategy in which to invest permanently, we recommend that your strategy be one that selects value stocks. However, the point of this book is that you should not just buy some investments and pray for results. Rather, you should adjust your investments to take the best possible advantage of prevailing market conditions.

Own Real Estate Through the Stock Market

Like the stock market, investing in real estate has for many been financially rewarding. Although it is possible to invest in individual properties, it is also possible to invest in real estate through the stock market. Companies that own and manage real estate are called real estate investment trusts, or REITs. Compared to owning individual properties, the costs of buying and selling REITs are far lower, and REITs are potentially safer because of the diversification they afford.

As of the end of 2006, the total value of REIT shares in the U.S. stood at $400 billion, which represents less than 3% of the value of publicly traded U.S. stock.[10] Even though REITs are but a small piece of the U.S. market, they should be an important part of your portfolio for two reasons. First, the long-term performance of REITs has beaten that of the S&P 500 Index when dividends are included for both investments. Second, REITs have been effective diversifiers of other stock market investments because their movements have often been uncorrelated with one another.

Figure 3.3 shows the long-term growth of $100 in a hypothetical index of REITs (the NAREIT Equity REIT Index) and in the S&P 500 Index from 1972–2007. (Figure 3.3 assumes the reinvestment of dividends, but does not take into account any taxes or transaction costs.) The compounded growth rate of the NAREIT Index was 13.4%/year, compared to 9.4%/year for the S&P 500 Index during the same period. The worst drawdown for the NAREIT Index was 37%, compared to 45% for the S&P 500 Index.

Figure 3.3 also shows that from 1998–2002, REITs and the S&P 500 Index moved in opposite directions: In 1988–1999, the S&P 500 Index advanced while REITs declined, but in 2000–2002, REITs advanced while the S&P 500 Index lost ground. A portfolio consisting of half REITs and half S&P 500 Index during the 1998–2002 period would have been safer than either REITs or the S&P 500 Index separately.

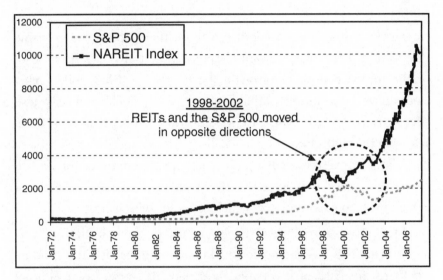

Figure 3.3 Hypothetical growth of $100 from 1972–2007 in the NAREIT Equity REIT Index and the S&P 500 Index including dividends.

Conclusion

Stocks have a long history of growth that has made them among the very best long-term investments. For individual investors not able or inclined to spend a lot of time researching individual companies, which is the case for most people, the diversification and potentially low transaction costs of well-chosen mutual funds and exchange traded funds (ETFs) make these the preferred vehicles to use in order to participate in the stock market.

We have discussed two ways of classifying stocks: by size and by valuation. Small company stocks have, over the years, been more profitable than large company stocks. They have also been riskier. A closer look at history reveals that small company stocks have their hot periods and lagging periods, either of which has lasted for years at a time. Ideally, rather than being in small company stocks all the time in pursuit of above-average returns, investors should emphasize small-cap stocks only during those periods when they are expected to outperform the broad market. In the next chapter, you will learn a simple way to do just that.

Stocks can also be divided into those that appear cheap (value stocks) and those that are more expensive than average because of bright future prospects (growth stocks). From 1969–2006, value stocks have been more profitable than growth stocks and have also been less risky. However, just as there has been greater profit in selecting the right time to be in small-cap stocks and the right time to be in large-caps, so too have there been opportune times for growth and other times when value was the stronger investment. Chapter 4 will address how to recognize which of these styles is best.

Finally, we saw that diversification has reduced risk without hurting returns. This has been true when comparing the risk in individual stocks to the risks of diversified portfolios of stocks (as in mutual funds and ETFs), and has also been true when considering broad areas of the market. The combination of an S&P 500 Index investment (such as SPY, the first ETF) with a small-cap value investment and a real estate investment trust has been an especially effective mix for reducing risk.

4

Nothing Succeeds Like Success

"The race is not always to the swift, nor the battle to the strong, but that's the way to bet."

—Damon Runyon

In the last chapter, we saw that within the U.S. market, there are several different investment styles, of which we highlighted four: large company value stocks, large company growth stocks, small company value stocks, and small company growth stocks. The reason why the distinctions between these styles are important is that at different times, different investment styles have performed the best. The rewards for choosing the better styles and avoiding the weaker ones have been significant. In this chapter, you will learn a simple strategy for keeping your money in relatively productive areas of the market, and how and when to switch your investments when necessary to stay on the right side of the market's major trends.

Most Investors Behave as if Past Performance Will Repeat Itself

It seems that almost any broker or financial planner who wants to entice you into a product that they are recommending will do so by citing good results in the past. At the same time, they will (or are supposed to, according to SEC regulations) tell you that past results do not guarantee any future performance. At the very least, they will place this important disclaimer in the fine print. Even authors of books that offer financial advice will tell you that past results do not guarantee future performance within the same volume as the advice itself, generally beautified by impressive records of past performance. So which do you believe: the past performance or the disclaimer?

Clearly, most of us ignore the disclaimer and instead act as if we expect past results to repeat themselves. One way to demonstrate this is to count the number of new mutual funds in an area, which is a reflection of public enthusiasm for investing in that area. Technology funds provide a clear example.

As of the start of 2007, there were 116 distinct technology funds. (Different share classes of the same mutual fund are not counted as separate funds.) Figure 4.1 compares how many of these 116 funds were started each year to the level of the Nasdaq Composite Index. (The Nasdaq Composite Index reflects the behavior of the prices of technology and other speculative stocks.) The figure shows, for example, that of the 116 technology funds now in operation, more than half (59 to be exact) were started in 1999 and 2000. It is clear that the largest number of technology funds were started after the market had already peaked (2000), while the fewest funds were started at what in retrospect turned out to be major market bottoms (1974, 2003).

Were the mutual fund companies relying upon a misjudgment about the stock market when they decided to launch so many new tech funds after tech stocks had already peaked? The answer is that the market of concern to them was not really the stock market, but the market for individual investors' dollars. Back in 2000, most investors believed that technology would remain a highly profitable investment over the long term and that the losses that year represented only a temporary setback. The fund companies responded to what their customers wanted by creating more technology funds.

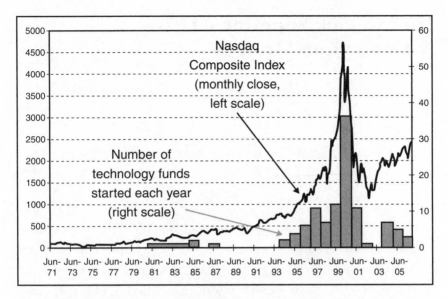

Figure 4.1 Nasdaq Composite and the number of technology mutual funds incorporated each year (from among those still in existence as of the start of 2007).

Although the technology sector represents an extreme example of a market mania, the overall message has been true in general: The average individual investor has not traditionally made good judgments about when to enter mutual funds. According to a study by Dalbar (2005 Quantitative Analysis of Investor Behavior), the average equity mutual fund gained 12.3%/year from 1985–2004, but the average mutual fund investor earned only 3.7%/year during the same period, presumably by selecting the wrong type of mutual fund at the wrong time.

The problem is that if you ignore past investment performance when making your current investment decisions, you are left with no guidance whatsoever. The solution, as I will show you in this chapter, is to utilize past performance in an analytical, systematic way. *If you limit the universe from which you select your mutual fund and ETF investments to well-established, well-diversified funds, it is safe to say that, historically, superior performance has tended to last more than one quarter at a time.*

How to Pick Superior ETFs—
A Momentum Strategy

"Everything should be as simple as possible, but not simpler."
—*Albert Einstein*

"Life is really simple, but we insist on making it complicated."
—*Confucius*

Even though chasing performance has often hurt individual investors, there is a kernel of truth in the expectation that what has beaten the market in the past could be expected to beat the market in the future. It turns out that well-diversified ETFs that have shown above-average performance during a three-month period have had a better-than-random chance of returning above-average profits during the subsequent three-month period.

This observation suggests a simple asset allocation strategy for picking winners: **Once every three months, you should select from among the best-performing ETFs from the last quarter to hold in your portfolio for the coming quarter.**

Our goal in devising an ETF strategy was to formulate the simplest possible strategy that would nonetheless afford readers the potential to outperform the broad stock market. Historically, in order to achieve this, you would have needed to consider only five basic equity investment styles, as follows:

1. U.S. large-cap value
2. U.S. large-cap growth
3. U.S. small-cap value
4. U.S. small-cap growth
5. International

The items in this classification are broad enough to be well-diversified, and therefore less risky than individual industry sectors. Yet at the same time, the performance disparities between these different styles have at times been large enough to generate significant added value compared to just buying and holding a fixed portfolio. All five of these styles are represented by ETFs with low expense ratios and generally low bid-ask spreads.

First Step: Select ETFs to Represent the Key Investment Styles

The first step is to identify a market index (and ETF) for each of these areas so that you have specific benchmarks against whose performance to compare. Table 4.1 lists the recommended benchmark index and ETF for each style, in addition to the ETF expense ratio, representative bid-ask spreads during quiet market conditions, and the relative long-term performance of the benchmarks compared to the average mutual fund with the same objective. You can see from the table that the ETFs available to track these five investment styles afford you all the advantages that ETFs can offer: low overhead, high liquidity, and superior performance.[1]

TABLE 4.1 Recommended Diversified ETFs and Their Benchmark Indexes

Investment Objective	Benchmark Index	Related ETF Ticker Symbol	ETF Expense Ratio	Bid-Ask Spread as % of Share Price[2]	% of Active Mutual Funds with Similar Objectives the ETF Would Have Beaten[3] 1997–2007
U.S. large-cap value	Russell 1000 Value	IWD	0.2%	0.01%	85%
U.S. large-cap growth	S&P 500 Growth	IVW	0.2%	0.05%	50%
U.S. small-cap value	Russell 2000 Value	IWN	0.25%	0.01%	64%
U.S. small-cap growth	S&P 600 Growth	IJT	0.25%	0.08%	77%
International equity	MSCIEAFE	EFA	0.35%	0.01%	57%

Second Step: Select the Two Top ETFs Every Three Months

The asset allocation strategy is very simple: On the last trading day of each calendar quarter, calculate the total return for each of the five ETFs in Table 4.1. (The specific steps for calculating total return are described in the inset.) Place your assets into the top *two* for the coming quarter (equal amounts in each).

For example, as of 3/31/2007, the first quarter total returns for the five ETFs are shown in Table 4.2. The first quarter of 2007 saw mixed returns for different investment styles. Small-cap growth and international stocks were the strongest two areas, so these ETFs (symbols EFA and IJT) would be the two selections for the second quarter of 2007.

TABLE 4.2 First Quarter 2007 Total Returns for the Five Basic ETFs

ETF	Investment Style	Ticker Symbol	1st Quarter 2007 Total Return
IShares Russell 1000 Value	Large-cap value	IWD	1.1%
iShares S&P 500 Growth	Large-cap growth	IVW	-0.1%
iShares Russell 2000 Value	Small-cap value	IWN	1.39%
iShares S&P 600 Growth	Small-cap growth	IJT	4.3%
iShares MSCIEAFE	International	EFA	4.1%

How to Calculate Total Return for ETFs or Mutual Funds

There are two parts to the total return of an ETF or mutual fund: First is the change in the share price (which can be a profit or loss), and second is the impact of distributions that the fund may have made. Distributions represent interest and dividend income earned on the securities in a fund's portfolio, as well as realized capital gains from any securities the fund has sold. Bond funds and

ETFs generally make monthly distributions, while equity funds and ETF make distributions less frequently.

As an example, consider the iShares Russell 1000 Value ETF (IWD) during the first quarter of 2007. The price per share of IWD on the last trading day of the quarter (3/30/2007) was $83.14, and the value on the last day of the previous quarter (12/29/2006) was $82.70. The change in share price is the price at the *end* of the quarter minus the price at the *beginning*, which in this case was a gain of $0.44.

Next, we turn to distributions. The distribution history for all the ETFs in Table 4.2 is available online at www.ishares.com. IWD made a distribution of $0.456/share on 3/26/2007.

The total return for IWD is the change in the share price plus the distributions: $0.44 + $0.456, for a total return of $0.896 per share. The percentage total return is the total return per share divided by the starting share price. In this example, the total return for IWD during the first quarter of 2007 was $0.896 / $82.70, which is 1.1%, as shown in Table 4.2.

Historical Results of the Quarterly ETF Selection Strategy

The five ETFs in Table 4.1 have not been around as long as the market indexes that they track, so the best way to get a picture of how this strategy might have performed hypothetically is to analyze index data.[4] Figure 4.2 shows the growth of $1,000 using the strategy of selecting the two most profitable benchmark indexes out of the five from the prior quarter to hold for the upcoming quarter, compared to the performance of each of the separate investments. (Taxes and transaction costs are not considered in these hypothetical results.) The recommended strategy consistently outperformed any of the separate benchmark indexes.

Profit is one goal, but risk management is also important. It turns out that the recommended strategy of selecting the top two indexes has been slightly safer than any of the individual indexes in addition to being more profitable. Table 4.3 shows the annual compounded returns from 3/31/1979–3/31/2007 for each of the five separate benchmarks and for the strategy of selecting the top two performers every quarter. Also shown is the strategy of selecting only the best of the five basic investment styles each quarter. Although the profitability is almost the same in both cases, we recommend selecting two out of five rather than just one investment style in order to achieve some degree of diversification. On average, the strategy of selecting the top two out of five benchmarks every quarter would have required you to switch one of your two holdings each quarter.

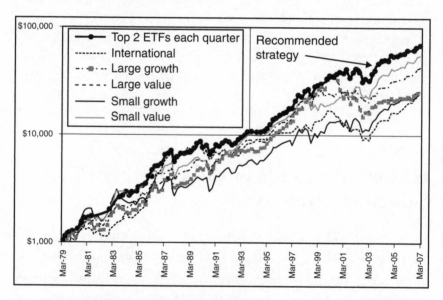

Figure 4.2 Hypothetical growth of $1,000 from 1979–2007 in different investment benchmarks and using the recommended strategy.

The quarterly ETF strategy is almost too simple to be believed: At the end of every calendar quarter, find the quarterly return (including dividends) for each of the five recommended ETFs. Place equal amounts of capital into the two out of these five with the highest returns and hold for the upcoming quarter. With this strategy, you do not have to predict which investment style will perform best—the market will tell you.

TABLE 4.3 Annual Gains and Worst Drawdowns for the Five Basic Investment Styles and Quarterly Selection Strategies

Investment Style	Annual Compounded Gain 1979–2007	Worst Quarterly Drawdown 1979–2007
Large-cap growth	12.2%	-57%
Large-cap value	14.3%	-27%
Small-cap growth	12.1%	-31%
Small-cap value	15.3%	-28%
International stocks	12.0%	-47%
Select top two from prior quarter	**16.2%**	**-25%**
Select top benchmark from prior quarter	16.4	-31%
S&P 500 Index total return	**11.5%**	**-44%**

Three-Month Strategy with Mutual Funds

The same approach that worked with a small group of ETF benchmarks has also worked with the much larger universe of mutual funds: Rank available funds at the end of each quarter based on investment returns (including dividends) and select the top performers to hold for the next three months.

This strategy was tested using information from the Mutual Fund Expert database. The universe from which the top mutual funds were selected consisted of all equity funds incorporated in 1985 or earlier that are still operating and that have at least $10 million in assets. 366 funds meet these criteria, including diversified U.S. equity funds, sector funds, and international equity funds. At the end of each calendar quarter, the gains/losses of each of the 366 funds were ranked, and then grouped into quartiles. The top 10% consists of the 36 funds with the greatest returns in the last quarter, and so on.

Remember to take capital gains distributions into account when evaluating fund performance. These usually occur during the fourth quarter (October 1–December 31), and result in a drop in the share price equal to the amount of the distribution. There are excellent resources available online for investors researching mutual fund performance, but if you are retrieving only share price data for the start and end of each quarter, you will almost certainly not get the correct total return for funds that have made distributions during the quarter. Yahoo Finance is a valuable resource, in part because it does attempt to adjust its daily price data to account for distributions, but as with any data source, the information is not guaranteed and omissions do occur regularly. (See the Appendix, "Internet Resources for Investors.")

You might wonder why the specific criterion of assets over $10 million was imposed. Our own judgment as investment advisors is that clients are best off in mutual funds of a substantial size. Otherwise, the portfolio manager is at risk for having his strategy derailed by large and untimely additions or redemptions to the fund. If shareholder additions or redemptions amount to more than 3% or so of a mutual fund, the manager is liable to have to buy or sell stock simply to deal with the cash flow. Under those circumstances, all the shareholders of a mutual fund will be burdened with transaction costs necessary to accommodate the actions of a small number of shareholders.

We restricted our study to mutual funds in operation since 1985 in order to include the October 1987 market crash in the research because that is a plausible worst-case scenario. (On October 19, 1987, the S&P 500 Index lost more than 20% of its value—the worst market crash since 1929.) That does not mean that it is necessary for a fund to have been in operation for 20 years before you invest in it. However, we do strongly recommend that any fund you buy should have enough operating history to show you how it fared when market conditions were not favorable. A rising tide may lift all boats, but it is not until the tide recedes that you can see who wasn't wearing a bathing suit.[5]

As a rough rule of thumb, the ten-year period (1997–2006) contains a wide variety of both favorable and risky market conditions for almost every flavor of equity mutual fund. If you are looking for funds that you intend to hold for years at a time, it is not unreasonable for you to limit your consideration to funds that have been around since 1996 so that you can see how they behaved during bear markets.

Results of Quarterly Fund Selection Based on Momentum

Figure 4.3 shows the growth of $1 from 1986–2006 invested in all 366 mutual funds, along with the results of investing in the funds in each quartile of returns from the previous quarter. Neither taxes nor transaction costs are factored into these hypothetical results.

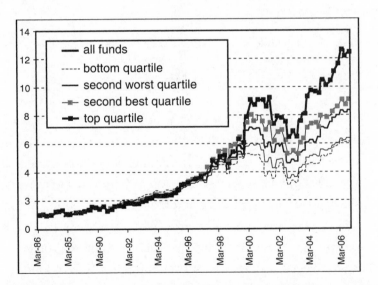

Figure 4.3 Investment growth of mutual funds based on prior quarter's relative returns.

It is clear from the graph that your assets would have grown the most if you had stayed in funds in the top 25%, and would have fared worst if you had stayed in funds in the lowest 25%. Table 4.4 summarizes the compounded gains and worst drawdowns for each of the fund groupings in Figure 4.3. Note that the average mutual fund returned 10.7%/year from 1986–2006, not matching the 11.4% annual compounded return achieved by the Vanguard S&P 500 Index Fund. This observation confirms the notion that index funds have outperformed a majority of (but not all) actively managed funds.

TABLE 4.4 **Results of Picking Equity Mutual Funds Based on Their Relative Performance in the Prior Quarter 1986–2006**

Fund Category	Compounded Annual Gain	Worst Drawdown
All funds	10.7%	-35.6%[6]
Prior quarter's top 10%	13.2%	-27.1%
Prior quarter's top 25%	12.8%	-30.0%
Prior quarter's second best quartile	11.2%	-33.9%
Prior quarter's second lowest quartile	9.4%	-40.5%
Prior quarter's worst quartile	9.1%	-41.4%
Vanguard S&P 500 Index Fund (VFINX)	11.4%	-43.7%

This fund selection strategy is simple and logical, so it is not surprising that it has worked over the long term. There is one more topic to discuss before you can start thinking about how to apply it to your own investments, however. The top 10% tier in the universe of funds studied contains 36 funds, and that is simply too many to purchase at any one time. Just as we do when we apply similar fund selection strategies to individual client accounts under $100,000, you will have to select a manageable subset of the top 10% of funds.

The easiest way to accomplish this would be to randomly select a small number (such as four funds) out of the top 10% available to you. However, random selection might not produce the optimal portfolio for you. Fortunately, there is an alternative to random fund selection that we recommend and use ourselves.

Typically, a large number of funds in the top 10% based on quarterly returns will be in similar areas. When technology was strong, the top performers consisted mainly of technology funds. More recently, in the 2000–2003 period, for example, small company value funds predominated; in 2004–2005, international funds were typically strongest; and in 2006, real estate investment trusts were disproportionately represented in the top ranks.

The first step is to identify which areas of the market are "hot." For example, our firm ranked a universe of 2941 equity mutual funds based on their performance through February 26, 2007. The investment objectives of the funds in the top 10% are listed in Table 4.5.

The relative frequency with which different investment objectives appear in the top 10% merits some further discussion. Consider that 9.7% of all funds have as their objective investing in mid-sized U.S. companies (U.S. midcap). Midcaps are companies whose shares have a total value in the $2–$10 billion range. In Table 4.5, only 4.5% of funds in the top 10% were U.S. midcaps. In other words, for this ranking period, midcap funds were less than half as likely to be among the top performers as one would expect to have occurred by chance. The implication is that for this data, the midcap sector was a relative laggard.

On the other hand, utilities funds constituted 2.4% of the best-performing group of funds, but only 0.8% of all funds. Therefore, utilities were three times as likely to make it into the top tier as would have been expected by chance alone (2.4% / 0.8% = 3). Real estate funds were another winning sector. Only 2.1% of all equity mutual funds are real estate funds, but such funds represented 18.5% of the top performers. As a result, real estate funds were nine times as likely to make it into the top 10% as would have been expected by chance alone.

TABLE 4.5 Probability of Finding Different Types of Equity Mutual Funds in the Top 10% as of the End of February, 2007

Investment Objective	Percent of Funds in Top 10% with This Objective	Percent of All Funds with This Objective	Relative Concentration of Funds with Objective in Top 10%*
Real estate	18.5%	2.1%	9
International/ global small company	10.3%	1.4%	7
Emerging markets	15.1%	2.1%	7
Telecomm	2.7%	.5%	6
Asia	6.8%	1.3%	5
Europe	4.8%	0.9%	5
Materials	5.1%	1.0%	5
Developed single country	2.1%	0.4%	5
Utilities	2.4%	0.8%	3
International/ global	13.4%	10.0%	1
U.S. small company	6.5%	13.4%	1/2
U.S. midcap	4.5%	9.7%	1/2
All-cap	1.4%	3.8%	0
Technology	0.7%	2.7%	0
U.S. large cap	0.3%	10.1%	0
Miscellaneous	5.5%	2.8%	2

*A number more than 1.0 means that the objective was more heavily represented in the top 10% than would be expected on the basis of chance alone, while a number less than 1.0 means that the objective was less likely to be in the top 10% than would be expected by chance alone.

If you can pick only a handful of funds, we recommend that your selections come from those sectors that were disproportionately successful in the most recently completed quarter. In Table 4.5, real estate, international small company, emerging markets, and telecommunications sector funds had the most concentrated appearance in the top 10% relative to their representation in the overall fund universe.

A portfolio comprised of the top fund (or least volatile fund) from each of these groups would represent an economical yet promising sample of funds expected to outperform in the coming quarter. Of course, when you select a fund for your portfolio, under no circumstances should you pay a sales load or purchase a fund that requires more than 90 days' holding, since you do not know at the time you purchase a fund whether or not you will want to keep it after you next re-evaluate your portfolio in three months.

By the time you read this, the sectors most disproportionately represented among the top performing funds could well be different than the sectors that were strongest at the time this was written.

How to Find Which Funds Are in the Top 10%

There is a handy, free Internet resource that allows you to rank mutual funds based on their three-month total returns (and by many other criteria): the "Deluxe Mutual Fund Screener" on MSN Investor.

To utilize the Deluxe Screener, go to http://moneycentral.msn.com/investor/home.asp. There is a list of links on the left of the screen. Click on the word "Funds." On the next screen, click on the link to the Deluxe Screener under the heading "Find Funds." You can use the screener to find the top funds as ranked by their three-month total return. Because there are over 12,000 equity mutual funds (which includes multiple share classes of the same fund), you can go down as far as 1,000 on the list and still be in the top 10%.

Diversification Is Important—Do Not Use This Strategy on Individual Stocks

We tested the results of selecting the best set of stocks based on the prior quarter's gains. Compared to mutual funds, the outcomes with stocks were disappointing. The only groups of stocks where outperformance in the prior quarter was associated with above-average gains in the subsequent quarter were large-cap value stocks. It was not possible to outperform indexes of small-cap stocks or of large-cap growth stocks by selecting the prior quarter's winners every three months.

Moreover, although it is possible to construct a well-diversified portfolio of winning mutual funds by choosing only three or four different funds, you would need a portfolio of some 20 stocks in order to achieve a meaningful level of risk reduction through diversification. The implication is that the simple procedure of ranking and selecting your investments every quarter has worked well for ETFs and mutual funds, but appears unsuitable to use in selecting individual stocks for your personal portfolio.

Conclusion

A simple but effective method of identifying the best ETFs and mutual funds entails ranking their performance at the end of each quarter and selecting the most profitable to hold for the subsequent quarter. Using this method would have kept you on the right side of major market trends that have favored particular investment styles for months or years at a time and would have increased the safety of your investments as well, compared to holding a fixed portfolio all the time. Moreover, the transaction costs of implementing this type of strategy have been modest.

5

Worldwide Opportunity

In the last chapter, we saw that it is possible to improve returns by moving into those areas of the market that are performing best. That strategy used four U.S. equity ETFs and only one international ETF: the iShares MSCI EAFE Index Fund, ticker symbol EFA. EFA represents the stock markets in economically developed countries outside of North America (mainly Western Europe, Japan, and Australia). EFA has the advantages of being easy to trade and having a low expense ratio. Its performance has been about in line with the average diversified international equity mutual fund.

But you can do even better, and this chapter will show two ways to improve your returns from foreign stocks. First, you can invest in a select group of broadly diversified international mutual funds with long, consistent histories of beating the market, reducing risk, or both. This is a one-stop approach to international investing. Second, for those of you who prefer a hands-on approach that is more opportunistic, we will show you how to utilize ETFs in order to gain exposure to those areas of the world that are showing the most promise at any given time. After a survey of the different opportunities available in foreign stocks, both strategies (one-stop shopping and active management) will be explained.

An Overview of the International Equity Landscape

The world is not flat. In other words, stocks in different regions and different types of economies do not all move in the same direction at the same time. The trick to international investing is to identify those areas where the opportunities are best. Just as we saw in Chapter 4, "Nothing Succeeds Like Success," that recent past performance of different investment styles within the U.S. could serve as a guide to where to invest in the near future, in this chapter we will see that the same approach can be used to guide your international investments.

In order to keep the task manageable, we will focus mainly on the three most important broad selections: Europe, Japan, and emerging markets. European stocks refer to markets in the economically developed countries of Western Europe. They are the largest group by market value outside of the U.S. We will see later that of all the major groups of foreign stocks, European stocks move the most closely with our own stock market. That makes them of relatively little use for diversification. However, there have been periods (most recently starting in 2003) when investors would have made significantly more money in European stocks than in American. The potential for greater gains at opportune times makes this group worth following.

Japan is the next largest stock market, and one with a very colorful history. From 1970–1989, the Japanese stock market boomed during what, in retrospect, proved to be a prolonged market bubble. After that bubble burst, Japanese stocks went into a 14-year bear market. As of October 2007, they have still not matched their old high of more than 17 years ago.

Japanese stocks are of interest now for two reasons. First, they have not been highly correlated with the movements of the U.S. stock market and therefore offer the possibility of risk reduction through diversification of investments in U.S. stocks. Second, Japanese companies are well positioned to take advantage of the explosive growth of the Chinese economy.

Emerging market countries are those whose economies and capital markets are still developing. They are a diverse group spread all over the world, of which the largest are South Korea, China, Taiwan, South Africa, Brazil, Russia, India, and Mexico. As a group, emerging market stocks have been riskier than stocks in developed countries, but they have greater growth potential.

The largest emerging market countries (in terms of the value of the stocks listed in their markets) are South Korea, China, Taiwan, South Africa, Brazil, and Russia. These countries account for 2/3 of the MSCI Emerging Market Index, with 15 other countries making up the rest. Energy and commodity producers make up 30% of the index; telecommunications, semiconductor, and other tech companies make up 28%, and banks make up 16%.[1]

In addition to the major groupings listed previously, the stock markets of Canada and Australia offer investment opportunities. Canada's economy is booming because of its production of natural resources. In particular, Canada has a rich store of tar sands from which it is possible to extract oil. Although the costs of doing so exceed the current market price of energy, should energy prices continue to climb, those tar sands alone could supercharge the Canadian economy for decades, not that it needs the help.[2]

The Australian market also benefits from high commodity prices, and its financial sector pays more generous dividends than its American counterparts. Moreover, the country is currently growing faster than the U.S., and the Australian government is not burdened by any significant debt.[3] Australia's economic fortunes are more closely linked to those of Asia than is the case of the U.S., so an investment in Australia is implicitly a bet on emerging Asian countries, but in a highly stable economic and political setting. Figure 5.1 shows each region's share of the world's total market value.

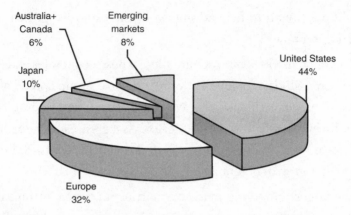

Figure 5.1 Percentage of total value of stocks listed in different regions of the world.

Now that you have been introduced to some of the stock markets around the world, the question should naturally arise as to how to take advantage of the variety of investment choices available to you. This chapter will present two different approaches. First, we have recommended a buy-and-hold portfolio of four outstanding mutual funds. Investors who do not want to take on the responsibility of following the market after setting up their portfolios can place their capital into these funds, which have excellent histories.

Following the description of the buy-and-hold portfolio, we present a simple strategy for shifting your assets among different areas of the world using ETFs, based on where the markets appear to offer the most promise. Whereas buying a diverse group of superior mutual funds is a form of hedging your bets, the ETF strategy offers potentially greater returns whenever one area of the world is particularly strong compared to the others.

Strategy 1—The One-Decision International Mutual Fund Portfolio

There are a small number of mutual funds with long histories of generating returns that have been high relative to the risks incurred during a variety of market climates. Although there is no guarantee of future performance, their past success in standing out from the crowd leads us to recommend four such funds in the international arena, as follows:

1. First Eagle Global (SGENX)
2. Tweedy Browne Global Value (TBGVX)
3. DWS Global Thematic (SCOBX)
4. New World (NEWFX)

The ticker symbols listed here correspond to the share class with the longest performance history. If you purchase any of these funds for yourself through a discount brokerage, you might have access to a different share class from the ones listed here. Because these funds are available without a sales load through discount brokers (except when a fund is completely closed to new investors), you should in no case pay a sales load to a full-commission broker or buy a class B share.

The first three of these funds invest in stocks from economically developed countries (mainly Western Europe, Japan, and Australia). First Eagle Global is a value fund that holds stocks mainly from developed countries including the U.S., but also from emerging market countries. The mix of holdings can be eclectic. For example, as of 3/31/2007, the fund's top holding was gold bullion, at 3% of the portfolio. Warren Buffett's Berkshire Hathaway was the second largest holding; 17% of the fund was in cash. This fund has managed to achieve returns that have been well above average (see Figure 5.2) while taking lower risks than the typical international fund. In fact, First Eagle Global has been consistently less volatile than even the S&P 500 Index. (International funds have usually been more volatile than the broad U.S. stock market.)

Tweedy Browne Global Value is another value fund that can invest anywhere, including the U.S. and in emerging market countries. As with First Eagle Global, the managers of Tweedy Browne Global Value have put together a portfolio that does not hew to any particular benchmark index. However, its portfolio differs from that of First

Eagle Global in that it has much less exposure to the U.S. and has a greater exposure to Western Europe. The largest countries represented in the fund's holdings are the Netherlands and Switzerland. The fund has largely avoided Japan.

The manager of DWS Global Thematic Fund (Oliver Kratz) has identified 12 investment themes on which he attempts to capitalize through his stock selections.[4] One of these is global agribusiness. The underlying assumption is that as living standards climb in China, India, Brazil, and other emerging market countries, the demand for food will increase. This will benefit companies such as Monsanto, which sells genetically engineered seeds to increase crop yield. Another theme is "talent and ingenuity," meaning that Kratz seeks out companies whose strengths arise from their intellectual property rather than from hard assets. Aside from companies in research-intensive sectors that you might expect (pharmaceuticals, technology), Kratz has included Porsche A.G. in this group. The fund has notable concentrations of its holdings in Germany and Brazil.

All three of the funds discussed so far have managers who are willing to deviate significantly from the major benchmark indexes. Informally, we have observed that the most successful managers have generally been willing to think outside the box without incurring extra risk. Figure 5.2 shows the hypothetical growth of $100 in First Eagle Global, Tweedy Browne Global Value, and DWS Global Thematic, and in two benchmark indexes: the performance of the average international equity mutual fund and the EAFE Index. First Eagle Global, Tweedy Browne Global Value, and DWS Global Thematic have all been more profitable and less risky than both benchmarks from 1999–2007.

New World Fund invests in emerging market stocks. Figure 5.3 shows that the New World Fund has been slightly less profitable than its benchmark MSCI Emerging Markets Index. However, New World Fund has been consistently safer than the average emerging market fund. As a result, when returns are balanced against risk, the New

World Fund is seen to have been one of the best emerging market investments available. One of the ways in which the fund has reduced its risk has been to include bonds and cash in its portfolio. For example, as of 4/30/2007, the fund had 15% of its assets in fixed-income or cash. Nevertheless, you should keep in mind that even this relatively safe emerging market fund has been significantly riskier than the broad U.S. stock market (as represented by the S&P 500 Index, for example).

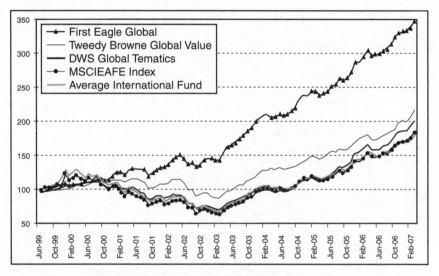

Figure 5.2 Hypothetical growth of $100 from 1999–2007 in selected developed-country international funds and two benchmarks.

With this short list of recommended funds in hand, all that remains is to decide how much to invest in each. First Eagle Global has had such an exceptional record that it warrants occupying the largest share—40%—of the capital you invest in international funds. The other two diversified international funds (DWS Global Thematic and Tweedy Browne Global Value) should each represent 15% of the capital you invest in international equity funds. We recommend that investors who wish to maintain a static portfolio allocate the remaining 30% of their international equity capital into New World Fund.

In Chapter 9, "The Definitive Portfolio—The Whole Is Greater Than the Sum of Its Parts," you will see that we recommend that a quarter of all equity capital be invested in international funds or ETFs, while the remaining three quarters should be invested in U.S. equity funds or ETFs. If you follow that advice, then your positions in the four equity funds will total 25% of your equity capital, as follows:

1. First Eagle Global: 10% of total equity capital.

2. Tweedy Browne Global Value: 3.75% of total equity capital.

3. DWS Global Thematic: 3.75% of total equity capital.

4. New World Fund: 7.5% of total equity capital.

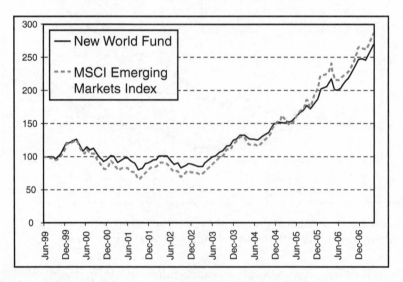

Figure 5.3 Growth of $100 in the New World Fund and the MSCI Emerging Markets Index, 1999–2007.

The Importance of Currency Exchange Rates

There are two factors that determine the return that an American investor receives on his investments in foreign stocks: changes in the stock price itself, and changes in the value of foreign currencies relative to the U.S. dollar. If you buy a mutual fund or ETF that holds foreign shares, those shares are priced in currencies other than the U.S. dollar. Just as the price of a foreign car gets higher in the U.S. when our currency falls, so too do the values of foreign stocks. **A decline in the U.S. dollar increases the returns from foreign shares. A rise in the U.S. dollar shrinks returns from foreign shares.**

As an example, there are two reasons why European stocks might outperform American stocks. First, share prices of European companies might be rising faster than the share prices of American companies. Second, the value of the Euro might rise against the dollar. Differences in currency trends are one reason why a particular part of the world might be a better investment for an American than another.

The performances of most international equity mutual funds are affected by changes in currency exchange rates. However, a small number of mutual funds (including Tweedy Browne Global Value) attempt to insulate their American shareholders from the movements of the currency markets. Shareholders in such funds will benefit when the U.S. dollar is strong, but will miss out on some potential gains when the dollar is weak.

Historical Performance of Different International Markets: Europe, Japan, and Emerging Market Countries—The Old World Still Packs a Punch

If you read the financial pages, you can learn all the ills that have beset Europe compared to the U.S.: sluggish growth, high unemployment, high tax burdens, powerful labor unions, high levels of government subsidies to local businesses, and government budget deficits. Yet, even though the U.S. prides itself as a bastion of free enterprise, European stocks have trounced ours in recent years, gaining 31%/year from March 2003–April 2007, compared to gains of 17%/year in the U.S. over the same period.[5] Figure 5.4 shows the long-term performance of European and American stocks. Notice that past major declines in the U.S. markets (such as 1973–1974, the October 1987 market crash, and the 2000–2003 bear market) affected European stocks as well, sometimes more severely.

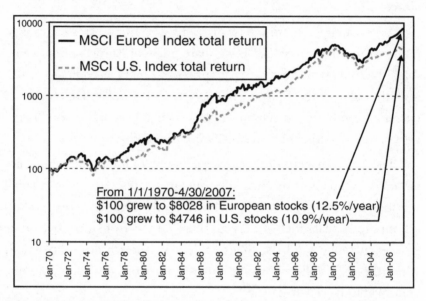

Figure 5.4 Hypothetical growth of $100 in U.S. and European stocks, 1970–2007.

Japan and the Rest of the Pacific/Asian Region: Two Very Different Stories

Any time you read a story about Asia these days, the theme is about rapid growth of China and India, their rising living standards, and the side effects these booming giants are having on the entire region. All of this is true, and there is little doubt that China and India will remain major engines of economic growth for years to come. Reflecting this economic landscape, Asian stocks have been extremely profitable since the start of 2003, gaining 22%/year compounded from the start of 2003 through the end of April, 2007. (During the same period, U.S. stocks returned 15%/year.)

Things were not always so bright for Asia. From 1989–2003, U.S. stocks were overall stronger than Japanese stocks. The Japanese stock market peaked in 1989 and went on to decline for more than 13 years, finally hitting bottom in early 2003. In contrast to Japan, markets in other Asian countries were quite strong until 1993. The entire Asian region suffered a major bear market in 1997–1998. Figure 5.5 shows the hypothetical growth of $100 from 1988–2007 in three indexes (including dividends but not taxes or transaction costs): MSCI Japan, MSCI U.S., and MSCI Asia ex-Japan. (Asia ex-Japan includes Asian stock markets, the largest of which are South Korea, Taiwan, Hong Kong, and China.)

The bottom line is that there is no part of the world that can be guaranteed to perform the best. Rather, the astute investor should look for the strongest areas and hold those for as long as they continue to be strong. As of 2007, Europe, Asia, and emerging markets are all stronger than the U.S., so you should maintain significant exposure to foreign stocks.

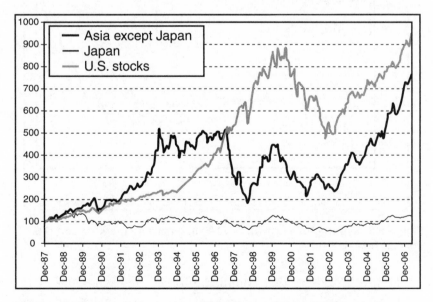

Figure 5.5 Hypothetical growth of $100 in Japanese, Asian, and U.S. stocks, 1988–2007.

Emerging Markets: The Leaders of Tomorrow

Emerging market stocks have returned 15.4%/year compounded from 1988–2007 with a worst drawdown of 56% (based on monthly total returns of the MSCI Emerging Markets Index). During the same period, U.S. stocks returned only 12.3%/year with a 46% drawdown.

A closer look at Figure 5.6 shows that gains in emerging market stocks have been far from uniform. From 1988–1994, both emerging markets and American stocks were profitable, with emerging market stocks by far the more profitable. However, from 1994–1999, U.S. stocks jumped even higher, while emerging market stocks actually suffered a small loss during the period. Emerging market stocks hit bottom in late 2001, some 18 months before the U.S. Since March 2003 emerging market stocks have risen much faster than U.S. stocks. (From 1999–2001, the MSCI Emerging Markets Index and U.S. Index performed similarly to each other.)

Figure 5.6 Hypothetical growth of $100 in emerging markets and U.S. stocks, 1988–2007.

Figure 5.7 shows that commodity prices and emerging market stocks have moved in parallel since the end of 1992. There are two possible explanations for this. First, commodity and energy producing companies are the largest segment of emerging stock markets. Second, growth in Chinese consumption is largely responsible for the rise in commodity prices. As a result, economic expansion in China drives emerging market stocks higher (in China as well as in Taiwan and South Korea, which are economically linked to China) and concurrently drives commodity prices higher. Although future investment performance cannot be guaranteed, Figure 5.7 would seem to suggest that a bet on emerging market stocks implicitly represents a bet that commodity prices will continue to escalate.

Figure 5.7 Emerging market stocks and commodity prices, 1992–2007.

By the way, you can get emerging market-like exposure without straying far from home. Canadian stocks have tracked the emerging markets quite nicely over the past 10 years (see Figure 5.8). This is not surprising given the make-up of Canada's stock market: 28% energy, 16% materials (mining, timber, and so on), and 18% banks, which more closely resembles the industry concentrations in emerging markets than in other developed countries.

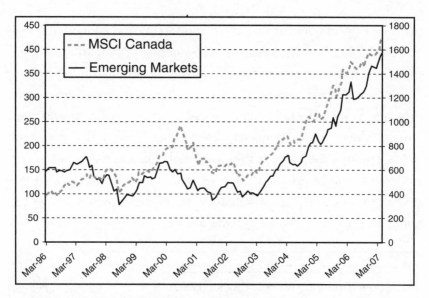

Figure 5.8 iShares MSCI Canada Fund (EWC) and MSCI Emerging Market Index, 1996–2007 (monthly total returns).

Diversification

Diversification improves investment performance if you are able to combine a group of holdings whose bear markets occur at different times. For example, bear markets in Japanese and emerging market stocks have not coincided with U.S. bear markets. As a result, these areas have been the best source of portfolio diversification. In contrast, European stocks declined during almost every major bear market in the U.S. since 1970—they have not been effective sources of diversification for U.S. stocks.

It is illustrative to compare the historical risk of a hypothetical portfolio of U.S. stocks to a portfolio of U.S. and emerging stocks from 1988–2007. During that time (through April 30, 2007), the MSCI U.S. Index made 12.3%/year with a 46% worst drawdown (monthly total returns excluding taxes or transaction costs). In comparison, a diversified portfolio of 80% U.S. stocks and 20% emerging market stocks (MSCI Emerging Markets Index) would have returned 13.2%/year with a 45% worst drawdown.

In other words, compared to owning only U.S. stocks, the diversified portfolio of 80% U.S. and 20% emerging markets was both more profitable and slightly less risky. The amazing thing is that by themselves, emerging market stocks have been riskier than U.S. stocks, yet diversifying an all-U.S. portfolio with emerging market stocks actually reduced risk. That is effective diversification.

Strategy 2—Three-Month Momentum Selection Strategy with Europe, Japan, and Emerging Markets

In Chapter 4, we saw that holding the investment style in the U.S. markets that returned the most in the prior quarter improved returns compared to holding a broadly diversified U.S. equity portfolio. It turns out that the same has been true when selecting from among the major regions of the world: Selecting the strongest region every quarter has been a more profitable strategy than diversifying broadly among international stocks.

Specifically, if you want to select your holdings from among the three major groupings of stock markets (Europe, Japan, and Emerging Markets), you should buy the one that performed most strongly during the prior quarter. At the end of each quarter, you should repeat your analysis and, if necessary, change your selection. Figure 5.9 shows the hypothetical growth of $100 from 1988–2007 if invested in a diversified portfolio of 1/3 in each major region compared to using the strategy of selecting the strongest region every three months. After 19 years, you would have ended up with twice as much money by following the active strategy compared to holding the average of the benchmarks.

Table 5.1 compares the results of utilizing the quarterly rotation strategy among the different international equity benchmarks (Far East, Europe, and Emerging Markets) from 1988–2007 to buy-and-hold strategies with static portfolios.[6] Utilizing the quarterly selection strategy for international benchmarks would have added 3.7%/year to your returns compared to the buy-and-hold strategy without any significant increase in risk.

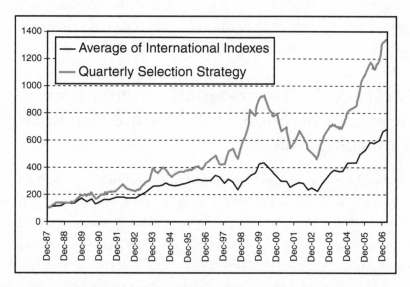

Figure 5.9 Growth of $100 using the quarterly selection strategy and in the average of the three broad foreign stock indexes, 1988–2007.

TABLE 5.1 Performance of the Quarterly International Equity Momentum Strategy and Passive Investment Alternatives

Strategy	Compounded Annual Gain 1988–2007	Worst Drawdown 1988–2007
Quarterly selection	13.5%	-50%
Average of international benchmarks	9.8%	-47%
U.S. stocks	12.0%	-46%

Selecting an investment alternative based on which has recently performed the strongest has worked best during periods when there were large, sustained disparities between different regions of the world. For example, 6/30/1997–9/30/1998 was a period when stock markets in Europe were strong, but stocks in emerging market countries and in Japan were very weak. The strategy would have kept you out of emerging markets during that difficult time. Instead of taking a 30% loss from 6/30/1997–9/30/1998 (the average of the market declines in Europe, the Far East, and Emerging Markets), you would have lost less than 6% as a result of being in European stocks for most of that period. The appeal of the three-month momentum system is that you do not have to predict which area of the world will be the strongest and which will run into trouble. The system will keep you where you need to be in order to capitalize on long-term trends. Conversely, during a period when there is no clear trend that distinguishes any one area from the others, the use of a momentum strategy will not be helpful and may even reduce returns.

How to Put the Three-Month Plan in Motion with ETFs

There are ETFs that you can use to implement the quarterly international equity momentum strategy in place of the benchmarks mentioned earlier, as follows:

1. iShares MSCI Emerging Market Index ETF (ticker symbol EEM).
2. iShares MSCI Japan Index ETF (ticker symbol EWJ) in place of the MSCI Far East Index.
3. iShares Europe 350 Index ETF (ticker symbol IEV) in place of the MSCI Europe Index.

The expense ratios of these ETFs range from 0.54%–0.75%. In addition to a mutual fund's or ETF's expenses, American investors lose out to withholding taxes that foreign countries levy on dividends paid to foreign investors. (The U.S. likewise withholds 30% of stock dividends paid to foreign investors in American stocks.) Stock transfer taxes can also be significant. For example, in May 2007, the Chinese government tripled its stock transfer tax from 0.1% to 0.3%. These taxes have taken an extra 0.6%/year off of the returns you would otherwise have gotten from holding European stocks. The impact of withholding taxes on emerging market returns has been 0.4%/year, but the impact on stocks in the Far East Index (mostly Japanese) has been only 0.1%/year.[7] The performance of the ETFs in real time (including distributions) will reflect foreign tax withholding. However the historical index data used in this chapter did not take foreign or U.S. taxes into account.

Conclusion

Although the United States has the most important stock market in the world, American equities represent less than half of global equity capital. Western European stock markets are the next largest group. European stocks by and large fluctuate in parallel with U.S. markets. As a result, they may be sources of added profit (compared to an all-U.S. portfolio) but are not likely to help reduce risk.

Asian stock markets have been less tightly correlated to U.S. markets than have European stocks. Asian economies and stock markets had their share of turbulence in the 1990s, but since 2003, Asia has been the epicenter of world economic growth, and its stock markets have climbed accordingly, growing far faster than U.S. stocks since 2003.

Emerging market countries are those whose economies are developing. Although this is a diverse group of countries, as a whole their stock markets have not been highly correlated with the movements of our own market (which is an advantage when constructing a diversified portfolio). Instead, emerging market stocks have been closely correlated with commodity prices.

A diversified international portfolio would include all of these regions. The easiest way to gain exposure is through high-quality mutual funds. We have recommended the following:

- First Eagle Global (SGENX)
- Tweedy Browne Global Value (TBGVX)

- DWS Global Thematic (SCOBX)
- New World Fund (NEWFX)

If you are able to purchase these funds without paying a sales commission, then a portfolio comprised of this group of funds could offer a superior balance between risk and reward if past patterns repeat themselves (which is unfortunately not guaranteed). Remember, do not buy class B or C shares, and do not pay a sales load. Of the four funds, New World and DWS Global Thematic should be considered relatively aggressive, while the other two funds were less risky than the overall international market during the 2000–2003 bear market.

Those of you willing to calculate the performance of three international equity ETFs each quarter and make quarterly changes to your holdings (if necessary) might be able to increase your potential gains by selecting the ETF that had the best gains during the previous three months. That ETF becomes your selection for the upcoming quarter. At the end of every calendar quarter, you repeat your evaluation and place your capital into whichever region was best in the prior quarter. The ETFs with which to implement this strategy are the following:

- iShares Europe 350 Index ETF (IEV)
- iShares MSCI Japan Index ETF (EWJ)
- iShares MSCI Emerging Markets Index ETF (EEM)

We will close the chapter with a comment on whether you should adopt the active approach of selecting the best ETF, or the more passive approach of holding mutual funds for the long term, hoping that they will continue to outperform their benchmarks in the future. Philosophically, we prefer the strategy of selecting the best international ETF each quarter because the rules to implement the strategy are objective and the motivation of following the prevailing major trend is easy to understand. Moreover, it is appealing to have a system by which to increase your exposure to the ETF that is performing best and to avoid any exposure to the weaker ones, as opposed to the passive strategy of maintaining a fixed allocation to a mutual fund even when its manager's investment strategies may be lagging. Although the international funds we have recommended have done very well compared to their peers, especially from 2000–2007, none of us knows how long the currently successful management teams will remain in place, or how the funds will fare the next time the market climate changes. If you can spare the effort, it seems more attractive to utilize a strategy that adjusts your portfolio so that your investments are in the optimal selections for whatever the market may be doing at the time.

6

Bonds—An Investment for All Seasons

"Loss of capital is a far more regrettable alternative than loss of opportunity."

—Kenneth Safian[1]

Bonds can play an important role in your investment program by providing a dependable source of income and can improve your overall financial safety by diversifying your other investments in stocks, commodities, and real estate. When you buy a bond, you know in advance what that income will be for the life of your investment, which is why bonds are considered to be safe investments. Also, unlike the case with stocks, you have a high degree of control over the level of risk you assume at the time you select your bond investments.

However, there is more to bonds than just safety and predictable income. There are areas of the bond market that have provided returns approaching those of the stock market with relatively modest risk. Other bond investments offer a U.S. government guarantee of income that exceeds inflation. In this chapter and the two that follow, you will learn about a variety of bond investments available to you, and the type of economic climate that is most favorable for each one.

We will also define important concepts you should find helpful in the selection and management of your bond portfolio.

How Much Should You Put in Bonds?

You will see later that there are many different types of bond funds available, including some that are appropriate for even fairly aggressive investors. However, in general, bond investments are safer than stock investments, and the older you are, the more you should put into bonds or other income-producing investments such as bank certificates of deposit or money market funds. Conversely, when you are just starting to save, you might want to have a rainy day fund of several months' expenses in a safe bond or money market account, but beyond that all savings might go into stocks. Table 6.1 presents some general guidelines for you to consider, although the exact mix of investments that is best for you depends on your specific situation and temperament.

TABLE 6.1 Suggested Allocations Between Stocks and Bonds at Different Stages of Life

Personal Situation	% of Liquid Investments in Bonds or Cash	% of Liquid Investments in Stocks	Comments
Just starting to save	All taxable savings should go into cash.	All retirement plan contributions should go into stocks.	You want to establish an emergency fund outside of your retirement plan. The goal for tax-deferred assets, which you should not access until you retire, remains maximum long-term growth.
After you have an emergency fund	0–25%	75%–100%	For funds that you do not need to spend sooner than five years, the goal is maximum growth. You have time to recover from market declines.

Saving for a house	75%–100%	0–25%	Funds earmarked for near-term needs (three years or less) should be in safe investments.
10 years before retirement	25%	75%	At this point, you should have a lot of savings to protect, but also a lot more to accumulate. You need to balance growth with safety.
Start of retirement	25%–40%	60%–75%	One or both members of a married couple can expect to live to their late 80s. That means your retirement savings have to last 20 years or longer, so long-term growth remains important, in addition to risk management.
Age 80 or older	40%–75%	25%–60%	At this stage, you can be conservative, although you still need to keep up with inflation.

Interest Income from Bonds— You Become the Banker

A bond is a loan that you, the investor, make to the borrower (also called issuer). In this regard, you are acting like a bank. Just as when you borrow money, at the time you take out a loan, you and the bank agree on an interest rate. So too with bonds: When a company issues a new bond to borrow money, it specifies the interest rate it is paying. In the bond market, the interest rate on a bond at the time it is issued is called the *coupon*.

Companies issue new bonds in units of $1,000. That means, in effect, that when you buy a newly issued bond, you are lending a company $1,000. During the term of the loan, you will receive interest at the coupon rate, and at the end of the loan, you will get your $1,000 back. The $1,000 amount per bond is called the *par value*, or *face value*. (The *Wall Street Journal* and other newspapers report the prices of selected, heavily traded bonds. Bond prices are quoted in "points," where each point is worth $10. Therefore, for example, a quote of 100 in the financial media indicates a bond price of $1,000.)

Suppose you buy a newly issued bond for $1,000 with a coupon rate of 5%. How much interest will you get each year? The coupon rate refers to the percent of the initial $1,000 price you will get in interest: 5% of $1,000 is $50, so $50 is your annual interest income. In the United States, bond interest is typically paid in six-month installments, so you will receive the $50 in interest due to you as $25 interest payments every six months. Note that for bonds with fixed coupons (which is most of them), the amount of the interest payment—$25 every six months in this example—remains constant throughout the life of the bond regardless of whatever fluctuations in interest rates may occur. This is the same as the terms on your fixed-rate mortgage: Whatever happens to mortgage rates overall, your payment on a fixed-rate mortgage remains the same (unless you refinance).

When you take out a mortgage, you agree not only on an interest rate, but also on the term of the mortgage. In the bond market, the term of the loan that bond buyers make to the borrowers is called the *maturity*. Maturities in the bond market have a wider range than mortgage maturities. Bonds can mature in as quickly as 90 days or less (commercial paper, Treasury bills), or as long as 30 years or more in the future.

If you buy a newly issued bond and hold it until it matures, that is all there is to the story: Pay $1,000, collect semi-annual coupon payments as your interest, and get your $1,000 back when the bond matures.

However, things do not generally work out that simply. In particular, most individual investors do not buy bonds when they are newly issued, but rather at some intermediate point in the bond's life. Most of you will therefore have to contend with bond market risk, the sources of which are primarily changes in interest rates and risks of default by the bond issuer. We will see shortly that a bond's maturity determines how much risk from potential changes in interest rates you are incurring. The shorter the bond, the safer it is.

Interest Rate Risks

Suppose you bought a bond for $1,000 with a coupon of 5%, which is to say that the annual interest income is $50. After you buy that bond, interest rates rise to 6%. That means that a $1,000 bond issued when interest rates are 6% will pay $60/year in interest. The first point to recall is that even after interest rates go up, the annual coupon payments from pre-existing bonds do not change. The bond you purchased for $1,000 still pays $50/year, even though a newer bond purchased for $1,000 would pay $60/year.

If you needed to sell your old 5% bond to raise cash, could you recover your initial $1,000 investment? Clearly, you would get less than the $1,000 you paid originally, when interest rates were lower. After all, who would pay you $1,000 for an investment paying $50/year when for the same $1,000, he could get $60/year elsewhere? Conversely, if interest rates fall after you buy a bond, your $50/year coupon payments would be higher than those available from new bonds. As a result, your old bond should increase in value above the $1,000 you originally paid for it.

To recap: Rising interest rates depress the values of existing bonds and bond mutual funds. Conversely, falling interest rates increase the values of existing bonds and bond mutual funds.

The extent to which bond prices change when interest rates change depends on the maturity. **The longer the term of a bond, the greater will be its price change in response to a move in interest rates.** To understand why, consider what would happen if you had bought a bond paying 5% for $1,000 (which is the usual issue price) and afterwards, rates rose to 6%. If the bond you bought happened to be short-term, maturing in three months, you will not have to wait for very long until your bond matures, and you can re-invest the principal at a better rate. You have missed out on higher rates for just ¼ year. On the other hand, if you had bought a 30-year bond, you would have to wait 30 years, a very long time, before you would have your principal returned to you to reinvest. The missed opportunity is significant, and as a result, the price of the long-term bond should fall more than the price of the short-term bond.

If interest rates happened to fall after you had bought your bond, the situation would be reversed. You would be enjoying above-market yields for just three months in the case of the short-term bond, which is not worth much economically. However, the holder of a 30-year bond could enjoy above-market yields for 30 years, which is relatively valuable. As a result, when yields drop, the values of pre-existing short-term bonds rise very little, while the values of pre-existing long-term bonds rise dramatically. Figure 6.1 shows this graphically.

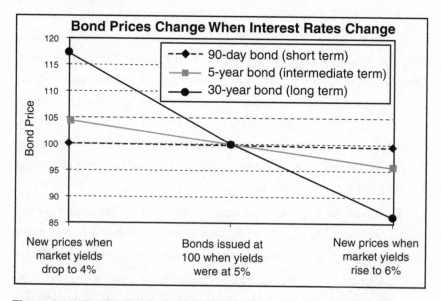

Figure 6.1 When yields change, longer-term bond prices move more than shorter-term bond prices.

The question naturally arises as to which maturity is the best to buy. The answer depends upon bond market conditions at the time, but there are some principles you can apply. Generally speaking, the longer the maturity of a bond, the higher the interest it should pay. This is similar to the situation with mortgages: the longer the term of the mortgage, the higher the interest rate. On the other hand, we have just seen that the longer the maturity of the bond, the greater the interest rate risk.

For most individual investors, bonds maturing in 5–10 years provide the best balance between the level of interest income and the level of interest rate risk. Long-term bonds—those maturing in more than 10 years—have paid little additional interest income compared to intermediate-term bonds—those maturing in 3–10 years. But the level of interest rate risk with long-term bonds has been much higher than the risks from intermediate-term bonds. Table 6.2 summarizes the different maturity ranges of bonds.

TABLE 6.2 Definition of Short-, Intermediate-, and Long-Term Bonds, and the Relative Amount of Interest Rate Risk in Each

Category	Years Until Maturity	Relative Interest Rate Risk
Short term	Three years or less	Low
Intermediate term	Three to ten years	Moderate
Long term	More than ten years (typically ranges from 10–30 years)	High

Yield to Maturity

The preceding examples imply that there are two sources of potential return from owning bonds: interest income and capital gains/losses based on the difference in the price you paid for the bond and its $1,000 value at maturity. The overall investment return of a bond held until it matures is a combination of these two and is called the *yield to maturity*. The yield to maturity is the most important piece of information that you need to know about how much a bond is slated to return.

When you read in the newspaper that interest rates are going up, what that really means is that the yields to maturity on existing bonds, and the coupon rates of newly issued bonds, are both rising. As we saw in the example of what happened to a 5% bond when interest rates jumped to 6%, rising interest rates drive the prices of existing bonds lower.

A Simple Strategy to Manage Interest Rate Risk—Bond Laddering

Recall from Figure 6.1 that if you think interest rates will go higher, you should buy short-term bonds or stay in the money market. If you think interest rates will go down, you should lock in current rates with long-term bonds. But what if you are not sure?

One simple solution is to split the difference by investing in bonds with a range of maturities. For example, you might put 1/5 of your bond money in two-year bonds, another 1/5 in four-year bonds, and so on up to the last 1/5 of your money in 10-year bonds. This type of portfolio is called a *bond ladder*.

In this example of a bond ladder, 1/5 of your portfolio matures every two years. If you don't need the principal, you should re-invest the proceeds from the maturing bonds into 10-year bonds. That restores your bond ladder to a portfolio in which 1/5 matures every two years. The evolution of a sample bond ladder is shown in Table 6.3.

TABLE 6.3 Evolution of a Bond Ladder

Start in 2008	In 2010	In 2012
$10,000 matures in 2010. (2 years)	**$10,000 matures now. Reinvest this in bonds maturing in 2020. (10 years)**	**$10,000 matures now. Reinvest this in bonds maturing in 2022. (10 years)**
$10,000 matures in 2012. (4 years)	$10,000 matures in 2012. (2 years)	$10,000 matures in 2014. (2 years)
$10,000 matures in 2014. (6 years)	$10,000 matures in 2014. (4 years)	$10,000 matures in 2016. (4 years)
$10,000 matures in 2016. (8 years)	$10,000 matures in 2016. (6 years)	$10,000 matures in 2018. (6 years)
$10,000 matures in 2018. (10 years)	$10,000 matures in 2018. (8 years)	$10,000 matures in 2020. (8 years)

Suppose you started your bond ladder with one-fifth of your capital in each of the following maturities: 2, 4, 6, 8, and 10 years. Under normal conditions, the 10-year bonds would pay the highest interest and the two-year bonds would pay the least. After two years, the two-year bonds mature and you reinvest the proceeds in 10-year bonds. That means that 2/5 of your portfolio consists of bonds paying interest at the 10-year rate: 1/5 at the time of your initial investment and another 1/5 at the time you reinvested the proceeds from the maturing two-year paper.

Every two years, the process repeats: One of your shorter-term original bond purchases matures and you reinvest the proceeds in 10-year paper with (usually) a higher yield than what bonds of the original maturity would pay. After eight years, you have a portfolio consisting entirely of bonds purchased with 10 years to maturity. The beauty of the bond ladder is that after the first cycle of turning over the short-maturity bonds with which you started, you end up receiving interest payments consistent with 10-year paper without ever having had to expose yourself to the full interest rate risk of holding only 10-year bonds.

Another advantage of a bond ladder is that you don't have to make a correct long-term prediction about interest rates. If rates happen to rise after you set up your bond ladder, you will get the chance to invest at higher rates in two years. If interest rates fall after you set up your bond ladder, you will have to reinvest at lower rates in two years but the rest of your portfolio was able to lock in higher rates at the start. Either way, over the long term, bond laddering will secure for you the average long-term rate of interest income with less risk than if you had placed all of your investment in long-term bonds at the start.

How to Tell if the Bond Market Is Safe

Utilizing a bond ladder can take the guesswork out of managing a portfolio of individual bonds. However, if you do not have enough money to invest in five different bond maturities (that is, $25,000–$50,000) spaced two years apart, then you cannot take advantage of this approach. (You usually have to pay a higher price to purchase less than $10,000 in any single bond issue than if you purchase at least $10,000 per bond issue.) Also, some investors by their nature prefer to swing for the fences rather than settling for a compromise strategy such as the bond ladder. Here is a simple strategy for deciding if interest rates are more likely to go higher or lower.

Reducing Interest Rate Risk While Keeping the Return

At the end of each month, check the Federal Reserve website (www.federalreserve.gov) for "Release H15-Selected Interest Rates." On the first business day of each month, look in Release for the latest monthly data on constant-maturity 7-year Treasury note yields. This number reflects the average interest rate on 7-year Treasury notes during the preceding month.

If the yield on the 7-year Treasury note is higher than it was seven months earlier, the interest rate trend is rising and you should have your income investments in the money market or in short-term bonds.

If the yield on the 7-year Treasury note is lower than it was seven months earlier, the interest rate trend is falling and you should have your income investments in intermediate-term bonds.

Performance of the Interest Rate Trend Indicator

This simple bond market asset allocation rule has reduced interest rate risk by more than half over the past 31 years. As an example, Figure 6.2 shows the growth of $1,000 in a broad U.S. corporate bond index (the Lehman U.S. Credit Index) compared to placing the same investment in the index only when the trend in 7-year Treasury note yields was favorable for bonds, and in the Vanguard Prime Money Market Fund when the trend in 7-year Treasury note yields was unfavorable for bonds. In order to make the results more realistic, 0.2%/year was subtracted from the results of the Lehman Aggregate Bond Index in order to approximate the performance of a bond index investment that is now available and which is discussed in more detail later in the chapter.

In Figure 6.2, the worst periods for the bond market are circled. It was during these periods that using the interest rate trend model would have protected you by directing you to move from bonds into money market. During the largest of these declines (in 1979–1980), bond investors would have lost up to 19% of their investment including interest. However, the worst loss using the asset allocation strategy was only 7%. The long-term profitability of holding the index at all times compared to switching between the index and money market is almost the same in both cases at 8.7%/year. However, these results do not count trading costs, which would likely subtract 0.2%/year from the active strategy. The active strategy made a total of 20 round trips between money market and bond index from 1976-2007, an average of one round trip every year and a half.

The bottom line is that the interest rate trend model has significantly reduced risk at the cost of only a small decrease in total return from hypothetical bond index investments over a 30-year historical period. The goal of this model is to protect your bond investments from the type of severe bond market declines experienced in the 1970s and early 1980s as interest rates climbed, while allowing you to participate in bond market gains when interest rates are stable or falling. Economic conditions since 2000 have been benign for investment-grade bond investors, but with energy, commodity, and gold prices all rising and the U.S. dollar near its all-time lows, it is far from certain that this will remain the case. The use of the interest rate trend model can help you protect your investment-grade bond investments even if the bond market climate deteriorates.

This active asset allocation strategy is suitable for investors who are concerned about the risks of a jump in interest rates and who can place the necessary trades without paying significant transaction costs. Later, we will describe the use of bond ETFs to implement this asset allocation strategy at potentially low cost. However, a good many of you might be able to manage your bond investments for free if you have access to both a money market (or short-term bond fund) and an intermediate-term bond fund in your 401(k) plans. Most company-sponsored plans do not charge you for switching your investments, and many would not restrict you from making the number of transactions required to implement this strategy. Conversely, if you already hold individual bonds, you will probably be better off holding them until maturity regardless of what interest rates do, since the costs (from the bid-ask spreads) of buying and selling individual bonds are prohibitively large.

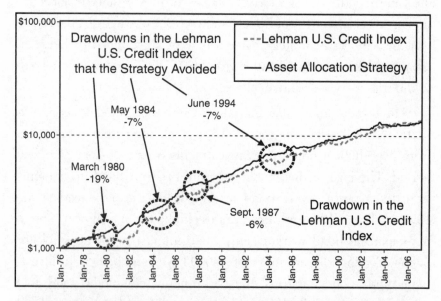

Figure 6.2 Growth of hypothetical investments of $1,000 in the Lehman U.S. Credit Index held continuously, or only when indicated with the asset allocation strategy discussed in this section. The most significant historical bond market losses are circled.

Implement the Interest Rate Model Using Exchange Traded Bond Index Funds

The inherent transaction costs make it impractical for individual investors to buy or sell specific Treasury bond issues whenever the trend in interest rates changes from falling to rising. However, there is a relatively new vehicle that allows you to invest in bonds at low cost and without trading restrictions: exchange traded bond funds (bond ETFs).

Bond ETFs are like mutual funds in that each share of an ETF represents proportional ownership of a portfolio of bonds. However, unlike the case with most open-end bond mutual funds, you buy and sell ETFs from other shareholders through a broker, just as you would trade shares of a stock.

There are two big advantages to utilizing bond ETFs to implement the interest rate trend model compared to using individual bond issues or investment-grade bond mutual funds. First, the internal expenses of the ETFs are lower than those of almost all investment-grade bond funds. Lower expenses leave more bond income available to you, and indeed, existing bond ETFs and the handful of low-cost investment grade bond funds provide the best levels of interest income.

Second, many bond mutual funds will not allow you to switch between them and the money market as frequently as the model might dictate during certain market climates. However, you can trade ETFs as often as you like because you, not a mutual fund, bear your own trading costs. Such costs include the actual brokerage commissions, which can be as low as $7 per trade, but also include the less obvious but sometimes more important expense of the bid-ask spread, a concept which was introduced in Chapter 4, "Nothing Succeeds Like Success."

For corporate bond ETFs, whose share prices are in the $100 range, the bid-ask spread ranges from one to ten cents per share under normal market conditions. That translates to a cost of 0.01%–0.1% per trade from the bid-ask spread. If you trade often, even a round-trip transaction cost as small as 0.1% can hurt your returns. Nevertheless, the ability to trade bond index funds at so low a cost is a great new opportunity for investors because the trading costs of bond ETFs can be lower than what even institutional fund managers pay to trade individual bonds.

Table 6.4 lists the bond ETFs that are likely to be most useful to individual investors in the future, including their expenses (all low), trading costs, and current yields. The iShares Lehman Aggregate Bond Index ETF (AGG) has been around since 2003. It is designed to represent the overall performance of the investment-grade bond market as a whole, which includes Treasury debt, mortgage-backed bonds, and corporate bonds.

The other ETFs in Table 6.4 are more specialized. The iShares Lehman 7–10 Year Treasury ETF (IEF) holds only intermediate-term Treasury notes. Although as a general rule, we prefer diversified bond ETFs to Treasury debt alone for individual investors (because Treasury debt yields less), if you do desire to hold Treasury bonds (perhaps because they are guaranteed not to default), IEF is the way to go.

The other two ETFs hold baskets of corporate bonds. The iShares Lehman U.S. Credit Index ETF (CFT) holds corporate bonds covering the whole range of maturities, while the iShares Intermediate-Term U.S. Credit Index ETF (CIU) is limited to the range of maturities that have historically offered the best balance between risk and reward. Note that these two ETFs were launched in 2007, and therefore have not yet demonstrated that they will be as successful as the other two bond ETFs in Table 6.4, which have been around since 2003. AGG, CFT, and CIU are all recommended for use in implementing the interest rate trend model described earlier. (Compared to the AGG, CFT, and CIU, all of which have corporate bonds in them, IEF has displayed greater day-to-day volatility and has a lower yield. These factors make it less attractive as a vehicle to trade on the interest rate trend model.)

TABLE 6.4 Recommended Investment-Grade Bond ETFs

ETF Name and Ticker Symbol	Type of Bonds in the Index	Expense Ratio	Bid-Ask Spread as % of Share Price	Current Yield-to-Maturity[2]
iShares Lehman Aggregate Bond Index Fund (AGG)	Sampling of all U.S. investment-grade bonds: corporates, Treasuries, and mortgage backed.	0.2%	0.01%	5.19%
iShares Lehman 7–10 Year Treasury Note Fund (IEF)	Treasury notes 7–10 years maturing in with fixed coupons.	0.15%	0.02%	4.61%
iShares Lehman U.S. Credit Index (CFT)	Sampling of dollar-denominated investment-grade bonds that trade in the U.S. (Mostly U.S. corporate bonds, but also includes foreign issuers.)	0.2%	0.11%	5.42%
iShares Lehman U.S. Intermediate Credit Index (CIU)	Same as in CFT, but only maturities ranging from 1–10 years.	0.2%	0.04%	5.23%

Investment-Grade Bond Mutual Funds

It can be difficult for small investors to buy individual bonds. As a result, for most investors, the best way to access the bond market is through ETFs or bond mutual funds. However, before you decide whether to invest in a bond mutual fund, you need to keep in mind the important difference between owning individual bonds and owning a bond mutual fund: Individual bonds have maturity dates at which you are assured of having your principal of $1,000 per bond returned to you. The implication for safety-minded investors is that even if interest rates move against you, if you are willing to hold your individual bond until maturity, you know what the stream of interest income will be, in addition to knowing when you will get your principal back.

In contrast, bond funds do not have a maturity date, and as a result, there is never any point in time at which you are assured of having your principal returned. Nor can you predict the level of bond interest income that the bond fund will distribute. The reason is that whenever cash becomes available in a bond fund as the result of interest income or the maturation of some of the bonds in the fund's portfolio, the fund manager will re-invest this cash in new holdings that he will purchase under whatever market conditions are prevailing.

From the perspective of maintaining a diversified long-term investment program, the lack of a single maturity date for bond funds should not deter you from using them. However, conservative investors looking for a predictable level of income with which to meet living expenses might be better off with individual bonds if they have sufficient capital to build a diversified portfolio in order to avoid too much exposure to the risks of any single bond issuer (besides the federal government).

Compared to almost all open-end bond mutual funds, ETFs have the advantages of low costs. In the investment-grade bond world, lower-fund costs have almost always translated into higher returns for the investor. However, there are transaction costs involved in buying and selling ETFs, so some of you might be better off dealing directly with a bond mutual fund that would not charge you anything to place your own transactions. For example, if you anticipate transferring an amount from every paycheck into a bond investment, a bond mutual fund would be the best option.

The average expense ratio for an investment-grade bond mutual fund is approximately 1%/year, which is high relative to the current investment grade bond yield of 5.7% (yield to maturity of the Lehman Aggregate Bond Index as of 6/29/2007). In addition, although a no-load bond fund would not charge an investor for buying or selling shares, the fund itself bears the transaction costs of buying and selling bonds for the fund's portfolio.

Most bond fund managers do not add enough value to make up the burden of this expense. In fact, the only bond manager who has performed well enough to overcome a 0.9% expense ratio has been Bill Gross in his Pimco Total Return Fund, class A, and his performance has been exceptional enough to make him a billionaire. The majority of investment-grade bond mutual funds have not matched the performance of the U.S. investment-grade bond benchmark (the Lehman Aggregate Bond Index) when both risk and profit are taken into account. As a result, there are only a small number of superior intermediate-term investment-grade bond mutual funds. All of them that we would recommend (aside from Pimco Total Return A) have expenses of 0.62%/year or lower.

You should never pay a sales load or buy mutual fund shares with deferred sales charges (so-called class B shares) in an investment-grade bond fund. Nor should you purchase class C shares in an investment-grade bond fund. (Class C shares, like class B shares, have built-in charges of 0.75%/year or more above the fund's usual expenses. These extra charges, called 12(b)-1 fees, reduce your return and are paid to the broker who sold you the fund.) No fund manager has been able to perform well enough to justify incurring the burden of these sales commissions.

There are, however, a small number of bond funds whose managers have consistently stood out from the pack over the long term. If you are inclined to buy and hold your bond investments rather than following the interest rate trend model that we recommend, you can avail yourself of some of our favorite investment-grade bond funds that are listed in Table 6.5. These fund managers have succeeded either in earning average returns with below-average risk, or taking average risks while earning above-average returns net of expenses.

TABLE 6.5 Recommended Investment-Grade Bond Mutual Funds

Mutual Fund	Ticker Symbol	Comment
Dodge and Cox Income	DODIX	Excellent long-term balance between risk and reward.
Pimco Total Return	PTTRX	High historical long-term returns compared to other investment-grade bond funds. Buy only the institutional class of shares or the class A shares without paying the 3.75% sales load (available through some discount brokerage platforms).
FPA New Income	FPNIX	Historically lowest risk of the funds in Table 6.5.
Vanguard Intermediate-Term Investment Grade	VFICX	Lowest expenses of the funds here, resulting in more income distributed to shareholders.

Conclusion

This chapter has covered three important concepts about investment-grade bonds that you should keep in mind when you are evaluating a bond investment—interest rate risk, time until maturity, and yield to maturity. All bonds (except for money market funds) have interest rate risk. When interest rates rise, the value of existing bonds and bond mutual funds falls. Conversely, when interest rates fall, the value of existing bonds and bond mutual funds rise. The longer the term of the bond, the greater the level of interest rate risk. Short-term bonds (three years or less until maturity) have very little interest rate risk, while long-term bonds (over 10 years until maturity) have high interest rate risk. For most individuals, bonds maturing in 7–10 years offer the best balance between the amount of interest and the amount of risk.

If you buy an individual bond that matures in 10 years, as its maturity date approaches, the level of interest rate risk on your bond shrinks. In contrast, bond mutual funds and ETFs have a portfolio of many bonds that mature at different times, and any time the fund receives cash (from a new investor or from coupon payments on its holdings), it will reinvest in new bonds. As a result, a bond fund or ETF has no maturity date, and the level of interest rate risk should remain fairly constant as long as the fund manager does not change the character of the fund's portfolio.

The yield to maturity (sometimes also reported as the "SEC Yield") is the single most important piece of information about the projected return of your bond investment. In the case of an individual bond, the yield to maturity tells you what your return will be if you hold the bond until its maturity date. In the case of a bond mutual fund, the fund portfolio's yield to maturity is an average of the yields for all the underlying bonds. It tells you what your bond fund would return to you if bond market conditions were to remain constant. Because bond market conditions do fluctuate, and since there is no single maturity date for a bond fund, the yield to maturity of your bond fund or bond ETF will change as bond market conditions evolve.

If you are concerned about the risks of a jump in interest rates, you should implement the risk-management strategy described here based on trends in the yield on 7-year Treasury notes. If yields are higher than they were six months ago, the interest rate environment is unfavorable for bonds (rates are rising), and you should be in a money market or a short-term bond fund. On the other hand, if the yields on 7-year Treasury notes are lower than they were six months ago, the interest rate environment is favorable for bonds, and you should be in an intermediate-term bond fund or ETF.

The best place to follow this strategy would be in a retirement plan that has no transaction costs, if such a plan is available to you and if it offers both intermediate-term investment-grade bond funds and a money market or short-term bond option. Otherwise, you can utilize the broadest bond market ETF (AGG) in a discount brokerage account.

However, if you are not comfortable tracking interest rates and moving around your bond investments, you would be best off in one or more of the exceptional investment-grade bond funds listed in Table 6.5.

As of this writing (November 2007), the interest rates available on investment-grade bonds are relatively low. In the next chapter, you will learn about other bond investments that have different risks and that, under some conditions, could improve your investment results compared to what you would achieve by limiting yourself to conventional, investment-grade bonds.

7

Special Bond Market Investment Opportunities

In the previous chapter, we discussed investment-grade bonds, which represent most of the U.S. bond market. You also learned a technique to identify when interest rates trends are favorable for holding investment-grade bonds, and when they are unfavorable. The biggest problem with investment-grade bonds as of mid-2007 is that the interest rates they are paying are relatively low by the standards of the past 25 years. There are two negative implications of historically low interest rates:

1. Even the most carefully selected portfolio of investment-grade bonds is unlikely to return more than 6%/year over the long term, because that is the level of current interest rates.

2. Because interest rates have far more room to rise than to fall, interest rate risk is as great as ever.

As a result, investment-grade bonds are very unlikely to return as much in the next 25 years as they did in the previous 25.[1]

In order to get potentially higher returns from your bond investments, you can turn to some special types of bonds that are less visible to the investing public than investment-grade bonds. This chapter will introduce four such bond niches: high yield bond funds, floating rate bank-loan bond funds, inflation-proof bonds, and tax-exempt bonds.

Higher Interest Payouts...
But Greater Risk

Up until now, the only risks regarding bonds that we have discussed resulted from the possibility that interest rates might move against you. However, there is another potential risk from bonds: the possibility that the borrower will not pay you the interest or principal that had been promised. That risk is called default risk. As you might expect, if you know at the time you buy a bond that the borrower has a significant risk of defaulting, you would demand a higher interest rate than if you were buying a bond from a financially secure company that has very little chance of failing to meet its obligations to its bondholders.

Bonds Have Credit Scores Too

If you watch TV or log onto financial websites online, you have likely heard advertisements asking you to pay to learn what your credit score is. The higher your credit score, the easier it should be for you to get a loan. It turns out that corporations that have issued bonds (or that plan to) also pay to receive a sort of credit score, called a credit rating. A credit rating is an assessment of the level of confidence that a company will be able to honor its obligations to pay interest and principal to bondholders when due. If financial conditions at a company change, the credit ratings on its outstanding bonds may change. There are three major firms in the U.S. that assign credit ratings to bonds: Standard and Poor's, Moody's, and Fitch.

The top credit rating applies to bonds guaranteed by the U.S. Treasury because the Treasury can literally print money if it needs to in order to pay the interest and principal it owes. Treasury debt amounts to approximately 30% of outstanding bonds in the United States. Below the risk-free credit rating of Treasuries, there a number of possible grades. (Personal credit scores are numbers, usually in the 600–800 range, but bond credit ratings are lettered.)

However, there is only one distinction of crucial importance for individual investors: investment grade versus below investment grade. Issuers of investment-grade bonds have rarely failed to make interest or principal payments on schedule. For example, from 1981–2000, the odds of the lowest-rated level of investment-grade bonds (a rating of BBB) defaulting were 0.22%.[2] That means that for every $400 in investment-grade bond holdings, less than $1 worth defaulted in an average year. Bonds that are below investment grade, in contrast, have a significant chance of defaulting. The long-term average default rate for bonds that are rated below investment grade has been 5%, although the default rate in 2006 was well below that, at only 0.8%.[3] Bonds that rated below investment grade are called high yield bonds or junk bonds.

Bottom line: We have already seen that changes in interest rates are one source of risk to your bond investments. Credit risk is another.

Not all defaults are equally harmful to investors. Some high yield bonds are backed by specific company assets (such as equipment). If specific company assets are pledged as collateral for a loan, the lender knows he will be able to recover something in the event of default. In contrast, most high yield bonds are backed only by a general obligation on the company to repay its loans. In the absence of specific pledged collateral, there is no guarantee that a borrower will have any resources available to satisfy its creditors in the event of a default. For this reason, asset-backed high yield bonds have historically lost less after a default than have high yield bonds without asset backing.

It is not necessary for a bond to default in order for bondholders to be hurt by credit risk. If a bond is downgraded, meaning that the risk of default appears to have increased, then the price of the bonds will likely fall. Conversely, if a bond's credit rating is upgraded, existing bonds will rise in value.

Just because a bond is rated below investment grade does not mean that it is a bad investment. High yield bonds are more likely to default than investment-grade bonds, so they must pay higher rates of interest in order to attract investors. Usually (but not always) the level of interest they pay makes high yields more attractive than investment-grade bonds. The trick to investing in high yield bonds is to be in the sector during stable market conditions (which is most of the time), but out of the sector during the steep declines that have periodically hit high yield bonds. You will learn how to do this in Chapter 8, "Treasure in the Junkyard—How to Tame High Yield Bonds."

In Chapter 6, "Bonds—An Investment for All Seasons; we state that only a relatively small number of open-end mutual funds have been attractive investment-grade bond investments, mainly because the expenses of most funds has outweighed the benefits that the portfolio management has provided. The high yield bond world is different: As a general rule, traditional open-end mutual funds are the best vehicles with which to access the high-yield area. Although we will see in Chapter 8 that there are some high yield bond funds that have excelled, even the average high yield fund has provided important benefits in terms of diversification and lower transaction costs that have more than made up for the funds' expenses.

Floating Rate Bank Loan Funds—A Special Kind of High-Yield Investment

"When in doubt, punt."—John Heisman

Floating rate bank loan funds are relatively new members of the retail mutual fund universe, but they have proven themselves to be excellent tools during periods of unstable interest rates. In the current environment of low interest rates that is prevailing (April 2007), the 6.5%–7.5% available from floating rate funds is very attractive. Table 7.1 lists the yields available from different types of bond investments, as well as the relative levels of historical risk.

TABLE 7.1 Recent Yields to Maturity and Historical Price Risks for Different Types of Bond Investments

Type of Bond Investment	Current Yield (Yield to Maturity)	Relative Historical Risk
3-month Treasury bill	5.0%	None
10-year Treasury note	4.65%	Moderate
Investment-grade bonds overall (iShares Lehman Aggregate Bond Index ETF ticker symbol AGG)	5.2%	Low-moderate
High yield bond fund	6.6%[4]	Moderate-high
Floating rate bank loan fund	7.0%	Moderate

If you have ever taken out a mortgage, you have probably noticed that every couple of years you have to write down a new address to which you mail your payments or address your inquiries. This occurs because the bank or investor that had originally lent you the money for your house decided to sell your loan to another institution, just as you might sell a bond that you hold in a brokerage account. There is a similar, but much smaller niche in the bond market involving bonds backed by adjustable-rate loans that banks have made to businesses. It is in this relatively obscure corner of the bond market that one of the best-yielding, moderate-risk bond investments is found.

There are 29 distinct[5] floating rate bank loan funds offered by 20 different mutual fund families. Of these, nearly half (14 of 29) were incorporated in 2002 or later, meaning that there is far less history for these types of funds than for most other types of stock or bond funds of interest to you as individual investors. The good news is that the earliest retail bank loan funds were launched in 1989, which gives us some glimpse into the pitfalls that might occur in the future.

The interest rates on the loans in which floating rate loans invest are adjustable, so there is no interest rate risk as there would be with a regular bond. In fact, if interest rates rise, you are better off because that will increase the amount of interest income paid to you as dividends. Moreover, adjustable interest rates tend to rise when inflation does, so this investment will probably not expose you to as much inflation risk as does a fixed-rate bond.

Credit risk is the main risk involved with floating rate bank loan funds. There is no guarantee that a corporate borrower will pay all the principal and interest due on a loan, nor that the collateral will be sufficient to cover its obligations. Earlier we mentioned high yield bond mutual funds—funds that hold bonds that have credit ratings below investment grade. The debt that bank loan funds hold tends to be from companies whose credit ratings are similar to those of high yield bond issuers. However, bank loans are generally better backed by collateral than high yield bonds are. As a result, when companies have defaulted on their debt obligations, holders of bank loan debt have fared better than holders of high yield bonds. (Generally, floating rate bank loan funds have at least 80% of their holdings in senior, secured debt. Senior debt is the first to get repaid in the event of a default, and "secured" means that there is specific collateral pledged to the repayment of the particular loan.)

Floating rate bank loan funds pay generous rates of interest compared to investment-grade bond funds precisely because of the credit risk. For example, as of early November 2007, floating rate funds are paying 6.5%–7.5% per year, which is 1–2%/year above what the typical investment-grade bond pays. In fact, yields are currently similar to what you can get from high yield bond funds, even though the latter have had significantly greater risk.

Floating rate funds vary widely with respect to the amount of risk they have experienced. The worst periods for floating rate funds occurred during the second half of 2002 and again in mid-2007. In 2002, the peak-to-valley losses in the value of floating rate funds ranged from 2% to 7%. From June-September 2007, losses in floating rate funds are ranging from 2%–4% but could extend further. Although there is no guarantee that future losses will not be more severe at some point in the future, 2002 was a period of low confidence in business, in which every type of corporate bond investment was punished for the sins of the stock market in general, and for corporate malefactors (such as Enron) in particular. The fact that a number of floating rate funds were able to weather that storm with only modest losses gives us some confidence in that sector.

There is one additional risk that these funds' price histories do not reveal. Unlike the case for mortgage-backed bonds, the market for bank loans is not very active. If one of these funds were to be hit with a wave of simultaneous shareholder redemptions, it could be very difficult for the fund manager to raise the necessary cash. As a result, bank-loan funds have various rules in place to protect them (and the funds' other shareholders) from the consequences of massive redemptions. Specifically, bank-loan funds require you to hold them for a minimum period, typically three months. In addition, many limit redemptions to specific dates of each month or quarter.

Lastly, bank-loan funds reserve the right to limit the total percentage of outstanding shares they will redeem at any one time. If more shareholders want to redeem than the fund allows, each shareholder gets only a pro-rata share of their request. For example, the Oppenheimer Senior Income Fund limits redemptions to between 5% and 25% of outstanding shares each quarter. The fund gives notice a few weeks in advance of how many shares they are prepared to redeem, and requires advance notice from shareholders as to how much they want redeemed. If the fund announced a willingness to redeem 5% of outstanding shares, but shareholders tendered 15% of shares for redemption, then each shareholder would get out of only one-third of his shares. Details are in the prospectus for this fund.[6] During the summer of 2007, some floating rate funds did receive more requests for redemptions than they were prepared to honor, so shareholders were not able to access their cash.

During periods of stable or rising interest rates, floating rate funds are excellent candidates for part of your portfolio. Table 7.2 lists some of our favorite floating rate funds.

**TABLE 7.2 Selected Floating Rate Funds with Current Yields
as of March 2007**

Fund Name	Ticker Symbol	Current Yield	Comment
Oppenheimer Senior Floating Rate	XOSAX	7.0%	Can only redeem on one specific date every three months.
Hartford Floating Rate	HFLIX[7]	6.5%	
ING Senior Income	XSIAX	6.5%	Can only redeem from this fund on the tenth business day of each month.
Highland Floating Rate	XLFAX	7.2%	Can only redeem on one specific date every three months.

As with any mutual fund, you should not pay an upfront or deferred sales charge in order to purchase these. Rather, utilize a discount brokerage house where these shares are available without sales charges (although modest transaction charges may be involved).

Which brings us back to the quote by John Heisman at the beginning of this section.... If you are uncertain about the market climate but want to earn potentially more than you could in a money market or bank CD, floating rate funds are a way to go. However, the restrictions on redeeming your assets from these funds once you invest renders these unsuitable for money to which you might need ready access on short notice.

The Safest Investment Anywhere—Treasury Inflation-Protected Securities (TIPS)

Inflation poses the greatest danger facing investors who depend on interest income from bonds to meet their living expenses because the level of interest income is fixed at the time you invest in bonds, but the purchasing power of that interest income erodes steadily. For example, if you plan your bond investments under the assumption that inflation will be 2%/year and it turns out to be 4%/year, you will either be able to spend less than you expected, or the purchasing power of your savings will erode faster than you expected. (Inflation has averaged 3.8%/year from 1952–2007,[8] which is more than most individuals are counting on for the future. At that rate of inflation, prices double every 18½ years.)

In 1997, the U.S. government offered fixed-income investors the ultimate protection from inflation. That year, the Treasury started selling Treasury Inflation-Protected Securities (TIPS)—bonds whose interest rate was not fixed. Rather, the interest paid by TIPS is reset every six months to be equal to the current inflation rate plus a fixed amount. For example, if you own a 2% TIPS, and inflation during the past 12 months was 3.1%, then the bond paid you 5.1%: the 2% fixed rate plus the 3.1% inflation rate.

TIPS pay this interest in two parts. The fixed, or real, component of the interest income is paid as cash coupon payments every six months. However, the inflation-related part of the TIPS return is added onto the bond's principal. In other words, unlike every other type of bond, the principal value of TIPS after issuance is not $1,000. Rather, the principal in a TIPS is $1,000 adjusted for the amount of inflation since issue.

The attractive feature of TIPS is that your coupon payments rise with inflation. To see why, let's look at an example simplified by the use of round numbers. Suppose you buy a TIPS at its issue for $1,000 that pays 2% plus inflation. At first, your cash interest payments will be $20/year. If there is no inflation, then your interest payments will remain $20/year.

Suppose that after a few years since the issue of this TIPS, consumer prices have increased 10%. Once this inflation is factored into the TIPS you bought for $1,000, its new principal value will be increased by 10% from the $1,000 purchase price, to $1,100. Moreover, the fixed interest payments will also increase. The fixed (or real) interest payment is calculated as 2% of the new principal: 2% of $1,100, which is \$22/year. Notice that both the principal of the bond and the rate of interest income have both increased by 10% since the initial purchase, because there has been a total of 10% inflation since you bought the TIPS.

Besides being inflation-proof, TIPS at many times can pay more than regular Treasury notes. For example, in late July 2007, a TIPS maturing in 10 years was paying 2.47% in cash interest plus the increase in bond principal to match inflation. At the same time, a regular 10-year Treasury bond was paying 4.79%. That means that if inflation during the coming 10 years averages 2.32%, the 10-year TIPS and the 10-year Treasury note will return the same. (The TIPS return would be the 2.47% interest rate above inflation, plus the 2.32% increase in principal to match inflation, which would total 4.79%.) During the 1997–2007 period, inflation averaged 2.6%/year, and that was a period of unusually benign inflation. Even if prices continue to rise as slowly as 2.6%/year, as a bond investor, you would get more from a TIPS at current market conditions than from a regular 10-year Treasury note. If inflation averages more than 2.6%/year (as we expect), then the advantages of TIPS would be even greater.

TIPS would be the holy grail of income investing but for two difficulties. First, very few of us can afford to retire solely on the amount of the cash interest payments that TIPS generate. As of this writing, TIPS are paying 2.47%/year plus inflation, which means that you would need \$1,000,000 in TIPS to get just \$24,700/year in interest payments that will keep up with inflation. As a result, most of you will not be able to rely entirely on TIPS to meet your living expenses without depleting at least some of your investment principal. However, to the extent that you might want to place part of your portfolio in safe investments that you do not need to watch, TIPS are an excellent choice.

Second, unless you hold TIPS in an IRA or other retirement plan account, you have to pay taxes each year not only on the cash interest payment but also on the principal adjustment. In periods of high inflation, a TIPS investor in a high tax bracket could paradoxically owe more money to the government than he received in cash interest. For example, if a TIPS pays 2% plus inflation to an investor in a 35% federal income tax bracket, what would happen to that investor after a year of 4% inflation? The total return on his bond would be 6%, of which 2% is received as cash and 4% is added to the principal value of the bond. The taxes due are 35% of 6%, which is 2.1%—more than the cash received. In order to pay his tax bill, the investor would have to have funds available from another source, or he would have to sell off some of his TIPS (which is most easily accomplished with a TIPS mutual fund).

The real problem with taxes is that they can easily turn TIPS from a guaranteed winner to a losing investment whenever inflation heats up. (The same is also true for a regular bond held in a taxable account.) For this reason, it is preferable to hold TIPS in a retirement account. Because of the expenses involved, we do not recommend holding TIPS in a variable annuity. In addition to buying individual TIPS bonds, there are two low-cost vehicles that hold TIPS: the Vanguard Inflation-Protected Securities Fund (VIPSX) and the iShares Lehman TIPS Bond ETF (TIP). Both of these have an expense ratio of 0.2%/year. Unless you are planning to trade TIPS to profit from the ups and downs of the bond market, we recommend the Vanguard fund over the ETF because there are no transaction costs with the Vanguard fund.

In deciding whether to purchase individual TIPS or one of these two inexpensive TIP investments, you should consider whether you want the security of knowing when your bonds will mature, which would favor individual bonds. On the other hand, if you want the freedom to make withdrawals from your bond account whenever you want, and in whatever amount, then the Vanguard TIPS fund (VIPSX) would probably be the best bet.

However, if you are looking for the ultimate safe investment as part of your portfolio and are not concerned about having current income in hand, individual TIPS could be best. The cheapest way to buy individual Treasury bonds (TIPS as well as regular bonds with fixed coupons) is through the Treasury Direct program, which allows you to buy newly issued Treasury debt without paying any commission. There is, however, an annual account maintenance fee of $25 for accounts above $100,000, and if you sell a bond before it matures, the government charges a fee of $34 for placing the trade with a dealer. (See www.treasurydirect.gov for the specific features of the Treasury Direct program and the dates at which new Treasury bonds are scheduled to be auctioned.)

Municipal Bonds—Don't Share with the Tax Collector

So far we have talked about bonds issued by the federal government and by companies looking to borrow money. State and local governments, as well as separate agencies that they sponsor, also need to borrow money from time to time. The big attraction to buying bonds issued by state or local governments, called municipal bonds, is that the interest they pay is generally not subject to federal income tax.[9] Moreover, if your home state has a state income tax and you buy bonds issued by a government entity within your state, you will probably escape state income taxes as well.

This can be very beneficial to investors in high tax states who are in the top tax brackets. For example, if your combined state and federal tax burden is 40%, a taxable bond paying 6% will generate only 3.6% interest for your benefit after you pay the taxes due. If you could get 4% tax-free from a municipal bond, then that would be a better deal for you, all else being equal. As a general rule, on an after-tax basis, municipal bonds tend to pay more than taxable bonds for high-bracket investors. If you are in a relatively low tax bracket, as many retirees are, then municipal bonds may not be for you. You should calculate the after-tax yields (using yield to maturity) from the different bond investments available to you before you commit to municipal bonds.

Are Municipal Bonds Right for You?

Here is a quick calculation you can perform to compare the yield on a municipal bond with the yield on a taxable bond.

First, figure out how much of each dollar of additional taxable interest income you will keep after paying federal, state, and local income taxes. For the average household, the burden of federal and state income taxes is about 30%, meaning that a typical investor keeps 70% of his taxable interest income after paying taxes.

Multiply the taxable yield by how much is left after taxes (0.7 in this example). If the result is higher than the available tax-exempt yield, the taxable investment is better. On the other hand, if the after-tax return on the taxable investment is less than the tax-exempt yield available to you, the tax-free investment is superior.

A specific example: Vanguard's Prime Money Market (taxable) pays 5.1%, and its New York Tax-Exempt Money Market pays 3.55%. An investor in New York state with a combined federal and state tax-bracket of 30% would keep $0.7 \times 5.1\% = 3.57\%$ from the taxable money market. This is slightly better than the 3.55% yield on the New York Tax-Exempt Money Market. If the same investor were in a 40% tax bracket, then he would get to keep only $0.6 \times 5.1\% = 3.06\%$ from the taxable money market, which is significantly less than the yield on the tax-free money market.

Unlike the U.S. Treasury, state and local governments cannot print money to pay their debts. As a result, just like corporate bonds, municipal bonds have credit risk and they generally carry credit ratings. Municipalities can buy insurance for their bonds. Insured municipal bonds carry the highest credit rating, implying low risk. However, in theory, insured municipal bonds are only as safe as the insurance company that guarantees them, which is good but not perfect.

There are a number of mutual funds that invest in municipal bonds. Although they afford excellent portfolio diversification and liquidity, their expenses are usually a big drawback. To see why this is an especially severe problem for municipal bond investors, let's return to the example of a taxable bond portfolio paying 6%/year in interest (yield to maturity) and a municipal bond portfolio paying 4%/year. Recall that an investor in a 40% tax bracket would fare better with the 4% tax-exempt bond portfolio.

However, if these portfolios are held by mutual funds with 1% expense ratios, then the yields generated for investors are reduced by 1% in both cases, down to 5% for the taxable bond portfolio and 3% for the municipal bond portfolio. The mutual fund's expenses represent, in effect, a tax of $\frac{1}{6}$ of the taxable bond yield (1% out of 6%), but a higher effective tax of $\frac{1}{4}$ of the tax-exempt bond yield (1% out of 4%). Net of the mutual fund's fee, the returns of the municipal bond fund are no longer better than the returns of the taxable bond fund on an after-tax basis. For this reason, we recommend that you utilize only the least expensive tax-exempt mutual funds—those with expenses of 0.3%/year or less. That pretty much limits you to offerings from Vanguard, or to the Fidelity Tax-Free Bond Fund (FTABX). Table 7.3 lists selected offerings from Vanguard that we have found useful in the past. Under current bond market conditions, the tax-exempt money market is the best bet because it pays the same yield as the other bond funds, but does not expose you to any interest rate risk. In addition to the funds listed in Table 7.3, Vanguard offers a number of funds holding bonds from single states that are designed specifically for residents of those states.

TABLE 7.3 Selected Tax-Exempt Bond Funds from Vanguard

Vanguard Fund	Ticker Symbol	Yield[10]	Expenses
Tax-Exempt Money Market	VMSXX	3.59%	0.13%
Short-Term Tax Exempt	VWSTX	3.52%	0.16%
Intermediate-Term Tax Exempt	VWITX	3.73%	0.17%

There is one exceptional municipal bond fund that we have used successfully for our money management clients over the years: The Nuveen High Yield Municipal Bond Fund (NHMAX). Even though its expenses are 0.88%/year, its performance net of expenses has been better than the low-expense offerings from Vanguard and far better than the average tax-exempt bond mutual fund since its inception in 1999. You should only purchase NHMAX without paying a sales charge to a full-price broker. The fund is available through discount brokerages such as Schwab and T.D. Ameritrade.

An alternative to tax-exempt bond mutual funds is to buy individual municipal bonds, for which you need to go through a broker. The process is murkier when you use a broker to buy bonds than it is with stocks because with bonds, there is no explicit commission. Rather, the price of the bond you are buying is marked up from the dealer's cost. Typically, the mark-up is 1–2% of the amount you are investing. If you buy a portfolio of individual bonds with an average maturity of 10 years, and you pay the dealer a mark-up of 2% in doing so, then you have effectively incurred an expense of 0.2%/year. This is less than what the vast majority of bond mutual funds charge. Although the Vanguard funds listed in Table 7.3 have lower expense ratios than 0.2%/year, the funds too must bear the impact of paying a mark-up to whomever sells bonds to them. (Presumably as large buyers, they should be getting a better price for their bonds than an individual investor could.) You should not take the 2% one-time cost for granted, however. At times, unwary customers have been known to pay mark-ups as high as 5%.[11]

The usual minimum amount you can invest in any single bond is $10,000 without paying a very high mark-up, so in order to diversify among several different bond issues, you would need a relatively sizeable portfolio (at least $50,000) compared to the $3,000 minimum investment required to get into the mutual funds listed in Table 7.3. You should also purchase only individual bonds that you are highly confident of holding until maturity, because selling bonds back to a dealer is like trading in a used car: In order for the dealer to make his profit, he has to pay you something below the true market price.

Here are some tips for investing in individual municipal bonds:

1. Ask the prospective broker for his proposed portfolio, its average maturity, its average credit rating, its duration, and its yield to maturity. Compare that to the similar portfolio characteristics for one of the bond funds listed in Table 7.3, which are available online at www.vanguard.com.

2. Be sure to specify when placing an order through a broker that you want to pay the minimum that his firm allows. (Brokers have a certain amount of discretion to lower the prices from their initial quote; for example, the price they might quote on a firm website.)

3. Sometimes bond dealers have what are called *odd lots* to sell. Normally, a broker wants to transact in round lots, which are multiples of 10 bonds. If in their inventory they have a smaller amount (say $5,000) of a particular issue, they might be willing to let it go at a lower price just to save themselves the trouble of keeping records on what for them is a very small investment.

For most individual investors, one of the recommended municipal bond mutual funds is likely the best way to go. However, issues for you to consider with regard to your own situation in choosing the best way for you to invest in bonds are listed in Table 7.4.

TABLE 7.4 Pros and Cons of Owning Individual Municipal Bonds Versus Municipal Bond Mutual Funds

Factors That Favor Using a Broker to Buy Individual Bonds	**Factors That Favor Using Bond Mutual Funds**
If you want a customized portfolio. (For example, if you live in a state for which an economical single-state municipal bond fund is not available.)	If one of the recommended bond mutual funds meets your needs.

If you want to know the exact income stream from your bond investments at the time you make them.

If you are concerned about the possibility of an alternative minimum tax liability. (Some interest paid by muni bond funds is subject to the alternative minimum tax. If you select individual bonds, you can avoid that pitfall.)

If there is no low-expense municipal bond mutual funds that meet your needs, and you have a broker you trust.

If there is a significant chance that you might want to cash out some or all of your bond investments before maturity.

If you have under $50,000 to invest in municipal bonds.

Surprise! Your Bond Is Gone. (Call Features)

If interest rates drop after you take out a mortgage, you have the option of refinancing to lock in lower rates. Some bonds, particularly municipal bonds, allow the borrowers to do the same thing. Such bonds are *callable*. Unlike your mortgage, which you can refinance at any time before the last payment, borrowers can call their bonds only at certain dates specified at the time the bond was issued.

Of course, the borrower will call your bond only if it is to his advantage. If interest rates are low on the call date, the borrower will return your principal to you, and you will be able to reinvest only at lower interest rates. On the other hand, if interest rates are high on the call date, the borrower will leave you with your relatively low-yielding bond. In return for these disadvantages, the investor in callable bonds receives more interest than he would receive from a bond without call features (all else being equal).

Do not be lulled by a high current yield on a callable bond. Before making the decision to invest, you need to know what your return would be in the worst case scenario that the bond is called. That return is known as the "yield to worst."

Different Types of Bond Investments to Suit Your Style

All bond investments are based on the basic principles we have covered so far. To review:

1. Bonds are loans that pay you, the lender (bondholder), interest during the term of the loan. At maturity, you receive the original face value of $1,000 per bond.

2. Changes in interest rates cause the values of existing bonds to change. A fall in interest rates increases the values of existing bonds. A rise in interest rates decreases the values of existing bonds.

3. A bond's credit rating is the assessment of a rating agency of its level of confidence that the borrower will be able to meet its obligations to pay interest and return principal to bondholders. Investment-grade bonds have relatively high credit ratings and a very low risk of defaulting. High yield bonds have below investment grade credit ratings, have a potentially significant risk of defaulting, and for this reason must pay higher rates of interest to investors.

Conclusion

Most investors can improve their balance between risk and return by placing 25% of their portfolio in different bond investments, both investment-grade and high yield. As with stocks, you can do well for yourself by selecting the right bond investments even if you choose not to adjust your portfolio once you set it up. The investments discussed in this chapter are excellent candidates for a buy-and-hold bond program.

As an example, Table 7.5 suggests a specific portfolio suitable for investors who do not want to tinker with their holdings once they get their bond investments set up. If your tax situation does not warrant holding municipal bonds, you can replace the tax-exempt bond funds in Table 7.5 with taxable alternatives: Vanguard Short-Term Investment Grade instead of Vanguard Short-Term Tax Exempt, and one of the bond funds recommended in Table 8.5 such as Pimco Total Return (class A or Institutional) instead of the Nuveen High Yield Municipal Bond Fund.

TABLE 7.5 Sample Buy-and-Hold Portfolio of Recommended Bond Investments

Bond Investment	Percentage of Buy-and-Hold Portfolio	Potential Risk Level	Comments
Floating rate funds (see Table 7.2)	20%	Moderate	Most have a short history, so the long-term risk is hard to project. The floating rate funds in Table 7.2 lost roughly 5% in June–August 2007.
Nuveen High Yield Municipal Bond Fund A (NHMAX)	20%	Moderate	Municipal bonds have been relatively safe in recent years, but from 1978–1981, municipal bond funds suffered losses of over 20%. Buy this fund only if you can do so without paying a sales load.
iShares Lehman Aggregate Bond Index ETF (AGG)	20%	Low-Moderate	This fund contains a mix of Treasury debt, federal Agency debt, and corporate bonds.
Vanguard Short-Term Tax Exempt (VWSTX)	20%	Low	This bond fund has not had a losing year since its inception in 1977.
Individual 10-year TIPS	20%	Low	If you hold a single TIPS to maturity, you will have no inflation risk and no default risk.

Investors who are willing to follow their bond investments can utilize the investment-grade bond ETFs (AGG or CIU) discussed in Chapter 8 for up to half of their bond investments, and can utilize floating rate funds and high yield bond funds for an equal amount. Even a bond investor willing to utilize the active strategy of Chapter 8 might want to place some capital into TIPS or munis for a really high degree of safety.

Unlike floating rate funds, high yield bond funds have for the most part been too risky to warrant holding them through thick and thin. However, high yield bonds usually pay more interest than even floating rate bank loan funds. (Market conditions in early 2007, when floating rate and high yield funds paid roughly the same, are exceptions to the rule.) Although no future results can be guaranteed, it has been possible to earn more than you would have from floating rate or investment-grade bond funds by utilizing high yield funds *if you were able to avoid the periodic, major declines that have occasionally befallen the high yield market.* In the next chapter, we will show you how.

8

Treasure in the Junkyard—How to Tame High Yield Bonds

"One man's junk is another man's treasure."

—Author unknown

In Chapter 9, "The Definitive Portfolio—The Whole Is Greater Than the Sum of Its Parts," we see that bonds issued by the riskiest borrowers, called high yield or junk bonds, pay higher interest rates than most other types of bonds. In this chapter, we will show you how to pick out those periods when you are likely to enjoy collecting the high levels of interest that high yield bond funds pay, and how to recognize those times when cash is more attractive. The goal is to achieve high yield returns with a level of risk similar to what you would experience in investment-grade bonds.

Because of their yields, high yield bond funds have often returned more than investment-grade bonds. For example, high yield bond funds have outperformed investment-grade bonds for four and a half years running (as of April 2007). Figure 8.1 shows the annual total returns for the average high yield bond fund and for the Lehman Aggregate Bond Index (investment-grade bonds). During this period, the benefits of being in high yield bond funds for a typical investor would have been even greater than might be inferred from Figure 8.1 because the performance of the average high yield bond fund is a good reflection of what an individual investor would have been able to achieve, while the performance of the Lehman Aggregate Bond Index does not reflect the actual expenses a bond investor would have borne.

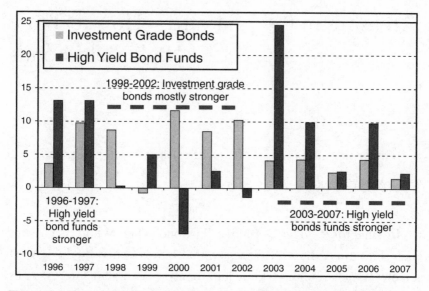

Figure 8.1 Annual total returns from the average high yield bond fund and the Lehman Aggregate Bond Index (a benchmark for U.S. investment-grade bonds).

The reason why high yield bond issuers pay higher interest rates is their greater credit risk, particularly the risk of default. When the business climate is deteriorating, high yield bond prices fall because investors tend to develop aversion to risk en masse, creating a temporary oversupply of junk bonds as everyone heads to the exits. The result can be poor performance despite generous levels of interest income. Figure 8.1 shows that during the 1998–2002 period, investment-grade bonds beat high yield bonds four out of five years.

In fact, the 1998–2002 period saw the worst underperformance by high yields relative to investment grade bonds since 1962 (the date of the earliest records in the Mutual Fund Expert database). The confluence of a number of factors contributed to the poor showing by high yield funds during those years. First, by 1998, after almost four years of calm in the high yield market, investors had become complacent and were willing to lend to risky borrowers for very little additional interest compared to what investment-grade borrowers had to pay. When the additional yield from investing in relatively risky bonds is modest, investors have every reason to dump their holdings at the first sign of trouble, creating a reservoir of potential selling pressure.

Second, during this period, the fear of deflation (falling prices) became an issue for the first time in more than 30 years. Deflation is a problem for any borrower because debt service obligations are fixed at the start of any loan, while falling prices threaten to shrink future revenues. High yield borrowers have less ability to withstand revenue shortfalls than investment-grade borrowers, so high yield bonds can be especially vulnerable during periods when businesses have difficulty raising or maintaining their pricing power.

Lastly, the failure of Enron and other formerly high-flying companies eroded investors' trust in business. As a result, corporate bonds throughout the rating spectrum were adversely affected in 2002, but high yields were hardest hit (compared to other businesses) because the riskiest borrowers depend most heavily on an environment of optimism and trust.

The first lesson to draw from Figure 8.1 is that during favorable periods, high yield bond funds can deliver very attractive returns. Although Figure 8.1 goes back only to 1996, the history of superior returns from high yield bond funds extends much further. For example, from 1980–2006, the average high yield bond's total return was 9.7%/year compared to 8.6% for the average investment grade corporate bond fund and 6.6% for the Vanguard Prime Money Market Fund. However, the potential downside of investing in high yield bonds is that during unfavorable periods, their risks can be significant (see Figure 8.2).

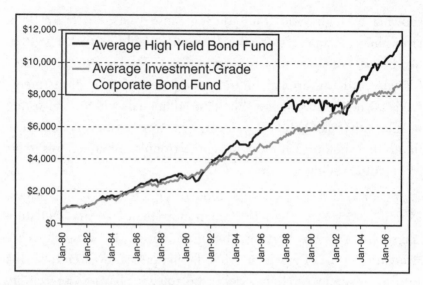

Figure 8.2 Growth of $1,000 in the average of corporate high yield funds and the average of intermediate-term investment-grade corporate bond funds, 1980–2006. (Source: Mutual Fund Expert database of 3/31/2007.)

Bond Default—The Big Risk in High Yield Bonds

Formally, a default means that a bond issuer is at least 30 days late in making a scheduled payment of interest or principal. What that really means is that the company and its bondholders have to negotiate over how much less than originally promised the bond-holders will ultimately receive. The good news: Bondholders have historically recovered an average of approximately 60 cents on the dollar from companies that have defaulted on their bonds. The probability that a high yield bond will default has varied widely from year to year, with a long-term average of 5%/year.[1] The actual recovery rate on defaulted bonds has also varied from year to year, but overall, a default has been far from a total loss.

As of this writing (July 2007), fewer than 1%/year of outstanding high yield bonds are defaulting. But in 2002, 16% of outstanding high yield debt defaulted in just that single year, and recovery rates were only 23 cents on the dollar overall—well below the average of 60 cents on the dollar.[2] Needless to say, investors with too much money in any of the one bond in six that defaulted suffered large losses that year.

How to Protect Yourself: Diversification

There are three strategies you can use to protect yourself from years like 2002. First, you should diversify so that your high yield bond investments are spread among many different issuers in different industries. That will mitigate your potential losses if bad fortune happens to strike particularly hard in certain sectors, as was the case with technology in 2002. Mutual funds offer the best vehicle with which to achieve diversification. You may have heard that index mutual funds (or ETFs) have outperformed the majority of actively managed mutual funds. Although this has been true in the stock market and in the investment-grade bond market, it is not true for the high yield bond market. In fact, although there are high yield bond indexes, there are currently no mutual funds designed to track any of them specifically. Individual high yield bonds have significant credit risk (as we have already seen) and also have high trading costs.

There is a high yield bond ETF (the iShares iBoxx $ High Yield Bond ETF, ticker HYG) that has the advantage of yielding more than most high yield mutual funds. However, with just three months of real-time history as of this writing, HYG appears to have greater short-term price volatility than most high yield funds. Although the prospects for this ETF appear promising, for now, traditional, open-end mutual funds are the best way to invest in high yield bonds.

Invest in the Best High Yield Funds

Second, you can limit your investments to only the best mutual funds. Not all high yield bond mutual funds are created equal. There are three high yield bond funds that have distinguished themselves by reducing their risk to levels well below the market average. We will list these funds for you and describe more fully their performance histories. Even if you had done nothing but limited your bond invest-ments to just these three funds, you would have done far better than most bond investors.

Respond to Market Changes

Third, you can monitor the high yield bond market on your own. When market conditions are favorable, you should increase your exposure to high yield bond mutual funds. However, when it appears that the high yield bond market is getting risky, you can reduce your high yield bond holdings and move assets into the money market. This chapter will explain how you can select the best high yield bond funds and how you can identify the best times to be in the high yield market.

The First Step in Managing Risk Is to Recognize It

We have already used drawdown to measure investment risk in previous chapters. Figure 8.3 illustrates some of the major draw-downs in a particular high yield bond fund (Waddell & Reed High Income/A, UNHIX) during the 1986–2006 period based on monthly total returns. This fund has had below-average risk since 1991, but did suffer a worse-than-average drawdown of 25% in 1989–1990.

When you are analyzing the investment performance of any bond mutual fund, and especially with high yield bond funds, it is impor-tant to take account of dividend income as well as price changes. For-tunately, Yahoo Finance provides historical total return data for mutual funds.[3]

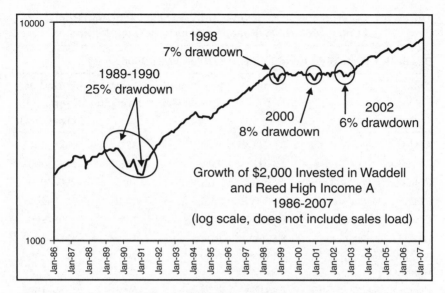

Figure 8.3 Growth of $2,000 in Waddell & Reed High Income A, 1986–2006, with four significant high yield bond fund declines noted.

How to Pick High Yield Bond Funds

Table 8.1 shows the historical compounded annual gains and drawdowns based on quarterly total return data for high yield bond funds selected because they had history extending back to 1980 or earlier. During this period, the average of these long-lived high yield bond funds returned 9.1%/year, with a range of 5.2%/year for the worst fund up to 11.3%/year for Fidelity Capital and Income. Risks during previous high yield bond bear markets have also spanned a wide range, from the safest funds (Lord Abbett Bond Debenture, Vanguard Hi Yield Corporate) that lost 10% at their worst, all the way down to the huge losses exceeding 40% seen during the worst times for Morgan Stanley High Yield and Aim High Yield. Some funds fared worse in the 1989–1990 high yield bond market decline, while others suffered more during the 1998–2002 tech meltdown.

TABLE 8.1 Returns and Drawdowns for the Oldest High Yield Bond Funds, 1980–2006, Based on Quarterly Total Returns

Results for High Yield Bond Funds, 1/1/1980–12/31/2006

Name	Symbol	Compounded Annual Gain	Worst Drawdown	Period of Worst Drawdown
AIM High Yield/A	AMHYX	8.7%	-42%	1998–2002
BlackRock High Inc/Ist	MAHIX	9.9%	-18%	1998–2002
Columbia High Yld Opp/A	COLHX	9.6%	-19%	2000–2002
Delaware Delchester/A	DETWX	8.6%	-40%	1998–2002
Dryden High Yield/B	PBHYX	8.6%	-16%	1998–2002
DWS High Income/A	KHYAX	10.7%	-18%	1989–1990
Eaton Vance Fund of Boston/A	EVIBX	10.4%	-18%	1989–1990
Evergreen Hi Yield Bd/B	EKHBX	7.5%	-29%	1989–1990
Federated High Inc Bd/A	FHIIX	9.9%	-18%	1989–1990
Fidelity Capital & Inc	FAGIX	11.3%	-25%	2000–2002
First Inv Fd for Income/A	FIFIX	7.9%	-26%	1989–1990
Franklin High Income/A	AGEFX	9.6%	-20%	1989–1990
Lord Abbett Bond Debnt/A	LBNDX	9.4%	-9%	1990
M Stanley Hi Yld Sec/D	HYLDX	5.2%	-58%	1998–2002
MFS High Income/A	MHITX	9.8%	-23%	1989–1990
Nicholas High Income/I	NCINX	8.4%	-19%	1999–2002
Northeast Investors Tr	NTHEX	10.8%	-12%	1989–1990
Phoenix High Yield/A	PHCHX	8.5%	-23%	1998–2002
Putnam High Yld Tr/A	PHIGX	9.7%	-16%	1998–2002
Van Kampen High Yield/A	ACHYX	7.9%	-27%	1998–2002
Vanguard HY Corp/Inv	VWEHX	9.7%	-10%	1989–1990
W&R Advisors Hi Inc/A	UNHIX	8.7%	-25%	1989–1990
Average of funds above		**9.1%**	**-23%**	
Results of equal-weighted portfolio of funds above, rebalanced quarterly		**9.2%**	**-18%**	

When evaluating high yield bond investments, just as with stocks, it is important to take into consideration the worst historical periods. The 2003–2007 (through July 2007) period has been very benign for high yield bond funds: defaults have shrunk to below 1% during the time, and investors hungry for yield have gobbled up record volumes of new high yield bond offerings that have been issued to finance leveraged buyouts. The 2003–2007 period, therefore, does not provide sufficient information on potential future risks and rewards. The worst periods for high yield bonds have occurred at roughly four-year intervals: 1989–1990, 1994, 1998, and 1999–2002. Figure 8.4 shows the average of quarterly returns from U.S. corporate high yield bond funds from 1986–2006. Clusters of losing quarters during the periods listed are readily apparent.

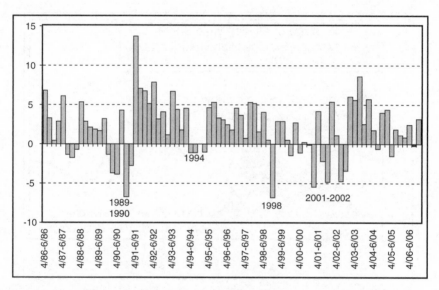

Figure 8.4 Average quarterly results from high yield bond funds (%), 1986–2006. Source: Mutual Fund Expert 2/28/2007.

Table 8.1 shows the extent to which different funds have had very different risk profiles. Morgan Stanley High Yield stands out as the most dangerous fund historically. In addition to its worst loss of 58% during the 1998–2002 period, it also tumbled almost 50% during the 1989–1990 bear markets. The fund's gains during favorable periods did not come close to compensating for its outsized losses during bear markets. Even Treasury bills, which have no risk, were more profitable than the Morgan Stanley fund during the 26-year period shown. Figure 8.5 shows the growth of $1 in the average of the high yield funds in Table 8.1, Treasury bills, and Morgan Stanley High Yield. The two largest declines (1989–1990 and 1998–2002) in the high yield bond market are indicated. During both of these declines, Morgan Stanley High Yield lost far more than the average high yield bond fund. As a result of these losses, Morgan Stanley High Yield returned less than Treasury bills from 1980–2006. **The moral of the story: Avoid high yield bond mutual funds that have displayed above-average drawdown. There will (usually) be other fish in the sea.**

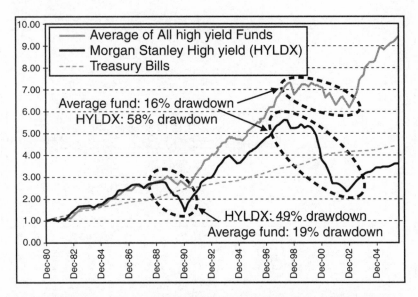

Figure 8.5 Growth of a $1 investment in the average of high yield bond funds, Treasury bills, and in the Morgan Stanley High Yield Fund (1980–2006).

Table 8.1 also has the results for the average of all the individual funds listed. As is frequently observed, diversification (with quarterly rebalancing) had a greater effect on reducing risk than it did on increasing return: The average of the funds' separate returns was 9.1%/year, while the hypothetical return of a portfolio of all the funds in the table rebalanced quarterly was 9.2%/year. However, notice that the historical risk of the fund average (18% drawdown) has been less than the average of the funds' risks (23% drawdown). The reduction in historical drawdown from 23% to 18% does not change a risky investment into a safe one. Nonetheless, removing more than a fifth of historical risk simply by diversifying is a big gain for relatively little effort.

The reason why diversifying among multiple bond funds has helped reduce risk is that high yield bond managers have different ideas about which bonds in which to invest. Some managers might prefer to chase yield by investing in the riskiest of junk bonds, while other high yield managers place greater emphasis on bonds just below investment grade in order to minimize risk. Some managers might see greater opportunity in casino companies, while others prefer to emphasize utilities or telecommunications companies. In other words, portfolio managers have different strategies, and so at any one time they will achieve different results.

Three Months to Success with High Yield Bond Funds

Because there is no guarantee that high yield bond funds will avoid future bear markets as severe as 1989–1990 and 1998–2002, we do not recommend simply buying shares in high yield funds and forgetting about them. Rather, we advise you to employ an active strategy that allows you to manage your investment risk. Fortunately, there is a very simple way for you to achieve this:

> **Monitor the quarterly results for each high yield bond fund you are in. If your funds have profitable quarters, you don't have to do anything for another three months. However, if any of your funds has a loss for the prior quarter, sell it and move the assets to cash until the fund has a winning quarter. As soon as possible after the close of a profitable quarter, move back into the fund.**

In other words, you need to evaluate your high yield bond funds only once every three months. Remember to take into account both price changes in your high yield bond funds and also income distributions the fund has made. Historically, income distributions have represented the larger part of the total returns. Most high yield funds make monthly distributions. However, Northeast Investors Trust, for example, makes only quarterly distributions.

Note that unlike the case with stock market indexes whose values are reported continuously throughout the day online, on CBNC, and so on, you do not know how your high yield bond has done on any given day until well after the market's 4:00 p.m. close. The table below has an example of the steps required to calculate the quarterly total return.

How to Find Quarterly High Yield Bond Data Online—An Example

Step	Comments
Go to Yahoo Finance (http://finance.yahoo.com).	
Enter ticker symbol next to "Get Quotes."	Type PBHAX (for Dryden High Yield).
Under the left-hand menu "More on PBHAX," click on "Historical Prices."	A data table will appear with default start and end dates.
Optional: Enter the start and end date for the calendar quarter just finished.	Start date 9/30/2006; end date 12/31/2006.
Look in the data table for the start date (the last trading day of the previous quarter). Note the share price.	Because 9/30/2006 was a Saturday (market closed), 9/29/06 will be the start date to use for the fourth quarter of 2006. On that date, the share price was $5.71.
Look in the data table for the end date (the last trading day of the quarter). Note the share price.	Dec. 31, 2006 would be the last day of the calendar quarter, but the last trading day was Dec. 29, 2006. On that date, the share price was $5.80, representing a gain of 9 cents/share.
If there was a decline in the share price during the quarter, you will also have to check distributions to evaluate whether the total return for the quarter was negative or positive. Distributions are listed in the body of the data table according to the date they occurred.	For PBHAX, fourth quarter 2006 distributions (per share) were 3.6 cents on Oct. 20, 3.5 cents on Nov. 21, and 3.6 cents on Dec. 21. Total distributions were therefore 10.7 cents/share.
Total return per share is the change in the share price (which could be a gain or loss) plus distributions per share.	The total return for PBHAX during the fourth quarter of 2006 is 10.7 + 9.0 = 19.7 cents/share, which is 3.45% of the $5.71 share price at the start of the fourth quarter.

Because the quarterly return was positive, you would hold onto the fund until you re-evaluate at the end of the next quarter.

If the quarterly total return had been negative, you would sell the fund and wait until the end of the upcoming quarter to re-evaluate.

Let's reiterate the risk management rule: Stay out of a high yield bond fund for three months following a calendar quarter with any loss (based on total return). Be invested in your high yield bond fund for three months following any profitable quarter (based on total return). Now we are ready to move ahead and see how well this simple system has worked.

You should apply this risk management tool to each of your high yield bond funds separately. For example, suppose that 50% of your high yield bond portfolio is allocated to Dryden High Yield (PBHAX) and the other 50% to Fidelity Capital and Income (FAGIX). You evaluate the total return of each fund following the close on the last business day of each quarter. If only one of the two funds has a losing quarter, you would sell only that losing fund, leaving 50% of your high yield bond fund capital in cash and the other half still invested. Similarly, if you had sold both high yield funds and only one of them had a profitable quarter, you would re-enter only that one profitable fund with only 50% of your high yield capital, leaving the other 50% in cash waiting for your second fund to generate its buy signal.

More Gain, Less Pain! Results of Risk-Control with High Yield Bond Funds

Figure 8.6 shows the average result of investing $1,000 in the high yield funds from Table 8.1 from 1/1/1981–12/31/2006, both on a buy-and-hold basis and when applying the risk management strategy to each of the funds. (There was no rebalancing between funds: The initial investment made in each fund on 1/1/1981 was allowed to grow within the fund.) **Not only did applying the risk management strategy to this group of funds cut the drawdown risk by more than half, from 16% to 7.5%, but return was slightly increased as well (from 9.1%/year compounded, to 9.4%/year).** These hypothetical past results include the benefits of money market interest when not in high yield bond funds, and do not include any allowance for transaction costs or taxes.

The number of times that the risk management strategy switched from high yield bonds to cash varied from fund to fund, ranging from 11 to 19 times during the 25½ year period. The average number of round trip switches from bond fund to cash and back was 15, or less than once every 18 months on average.

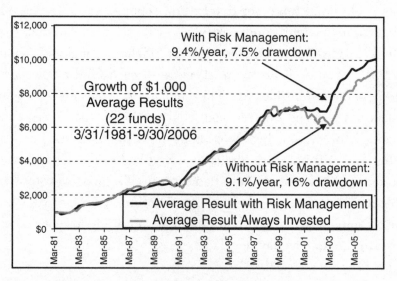

Figure 8.6 Average results of investing $1,000 in the high yield bond funds from Table 8.1, with and without risk management.

As a general rule, the more high yield bond funds you can utilize, the safer the bond program will be. However, it is not necessary to use more than one high yield bond fund, and in some cases, it may not even be possible. Many individual investors will want to utilize high yield bond funds in a company-sponsored 401(k) or 403(b) plan. In those plans, there is rarely more than one high yield bond fund from which to choose. Alternatively, if you use a discount brokerage mutual fund platform such as Schwab's or T.D. Ameritrade's, you may have to pay a transaction fee (generally around $24) for every mutual fund you purchase. Obviously, tracking many separate high yield bond funds will multiply your transaction costs.

The good news is that the risk management strategy described here would have worked with most mutual funds. Even if the only fund available to you had been the riskiest one in Table 8.1 (Morgan Stanley High Yield), the risk management technique would have produced good results. Figure 8.7 shows that on a buy-and-hold basis, from 1981–2006, Morgan Stanley High Yield returned only 5.2%/year with a 58% drawdown (see Table 8.1). However, had the risk management strategy been utilized, the return from this fund would have been 10.1%/year with only 10% drawdown.

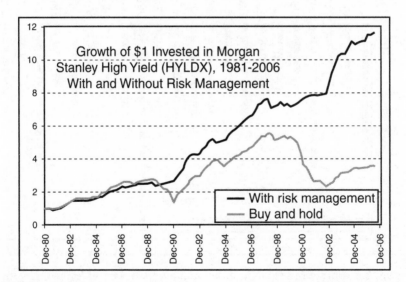

Figure 8.7 Morgan Stanley High Yield (HYLDX), 1981–2006, with and without risk management.

The risk management strategy reduced the drawdowns of the funds in Table 8.1 by more than half from 24% to under 10% on average.

Figure 8.8 shows the risk reduction achieved that each of the 22 funds in Table 8.1 would have experienced from 1981–2006. The results show that of the 22 funds:

- Three funds were historically safe with or without risk management (Northeast Investors Trust, Vanguard High Yield Corporate, and Lord Abbett Bond Debenture), having experienced the worst drawdowns of only 9–12% during the 1981–2006 period.
- 17 funds had their drawdowns significantly reduced through the application of the risk control strategy, from a drawdown of 26% to less than 10%.
- There were only two funds out of the 22 in Table 8.1 whose worst drawdowns remained higher than 12% using the risk management strategy here: BlackRock High Yield (MAHIX) and Columbia High Yield (COLHX).

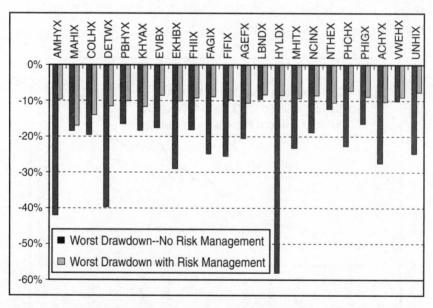

Figure 8.8 Worst drawdown in individual high yield bond funds (1981–2006), with versus without risk management.

The reduction in risk that you could have achieved did not come at the expense of returns overall. Figure 8.9 shows the 1981–2006 compounded annual gains for each of these funds, with and without risk management. With nine out of the 22 funds, the use of risk management increased return, whereas with 13 out of 22 risk management reduced return, albeit by small amounts. The average of all 22 funds gained 9.1%/year with 16% drawdown in the absence of risk management. Had the risk management strategy been applied, the results would have been a gain of 9.4%/year with 7.5% drawdown.

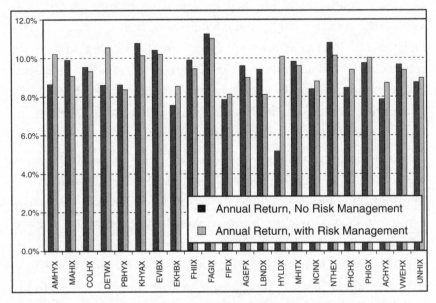

Figure 8.9 There is no overall loss of return from utilizing the risk management strategy in individual high yield bond funds (1981–2006).

With some funds (especially the riskiest ones), profitability was actually improved as a byproduct of managing risk. This strategy will allow you to take advantage of high yield bond fund offerings in your company retirement plans, where there are no transaction costs or tax consequences to cashing out of the fund following negative quarters.

Just to summarize the results for the three-month risk management strategy: Based on the 1981–2006 performance history of the funds studied, on average more than half of the drawdown risk was eliminated using the strategy with no overall loss of return compared to remaining invested all the time.

Three Special High Yield Bond Funds

The three safest funds in Table 8.1 deserve special mention: Northeast Investors Trust (NTHEX), Vanguard High Yield Corporate (VWEHX), and Lord Abbett Bond Debenture (LBNDX). These funds have had among the lowest risks of all U.S. high yield bond funds in the comprehensive Mutual Fund Expert database. If you had been continuously invested in any of these three funds from 1981–2006, your drawdown would have ranged from 9–12%. Using the high yield timing model presented here would not have improved the returns or the already relatively low levels of risk entailed in holding any of these three funds. On a buy-and-hold basis, these three funds performed similarly to high yield bond funds handled using the recommended timing model.

As with any investment, there is no guarantee that these funds will remain as safe as they were in the past. If you believe that these funds will be able to continue their past safety records, you might consider taking permanent positions with some of your bond capital. In fact, Vanguard High Yield has a minimum one-year holding period, so if you want to invest in that fund, you should plan to do so on a permanent basis. If you do commit your money to these funds, you should at the very least keep an eye on them and be ready to exit if they demonstrate worse behavior (greater losses) than they have historically.

One more note about buying these funds: Northeast Investors Trust and Vanguard High Yield Corporate are no-load funds, so you can deal directly with the fund companies if you like, or invest in it through your favorite brokerage platform if their charges are reasonable.[4] Lord Abbett Bond Debenture is a load fund, meaning that if you were to buy it through a commission broker, you would lose several percent of your investment as sales charges. You should not invest in Lord Abbett Bond Debenture except through a discount brokerage firm that allows you to buy shares without an upfront sales charge. (Never buy the class B or C shares.)

Conclusion

"The future isn't what it used to be."

—Yogi Berra[5]

We doubt that Yogi Berra was referring to the bond market, but his observation certainly applies now because the high yield bond market (and the bond market generally) appears to be in a position of above-average risk as of April 2007.

High yield bond yields are at historically low levels, with high yield bond benchmarks now paying approximately 7%/year.[6] High yield bond mutual fund yields to maturity (net of the funds' expenses) span a wide range (from below 6% to 8%), although a majority are paying 6.5%–7.25%. This is well below the long-term average yield of over 9% seen in high yield bond funds from 1983–2007.[7]

A second measure of the potential risk of high yield bonds is the difference between the yield they are paying and the yield you could get from investment-grade bonds. This difference is called a *spread*. The spread between investment grade and high yield bonds, at 2%, is as low as it has ever been in the past 20 years.[8] It is hard to conceive of things getting better for the bond market, but unfortunately, there is a lot of room for conditions to worsen. For that reason, we are attracted to the concept of the active risk management strategy that you can apply to high yield bond funds. The hope is that even if bond market conditions worsen, the damage will be limited and, using the strategy, you will have some guidance as to when to be in high yield bond funds and when to be in cash.

In summary: The high yield bond strategy involves placing capital in one or more high yield bond funds available to you. You manage your high yield portfolio by checking the returns as of the last day of each quarter. If your fund showed a loss, you move to cash for the upcoming quarter and re-evaluate in three months. You stay in cash until your fund shows a positive quarter, at which point you move the assets back into your high yield bond fund. Adhering to this strategy in the past would have reduced your risk by more than half while marginally boosting returns.

Appendix to Chapter 8: How to Download Total Return Data from Yahoo Finance

1. Get to the Yahoo Finance home page at http://finance.yahoo.com.

2. Enter the ticker symbol for the mutual fund next to the "Get Quotes" button.

3. After you retrieve the latest daily quote, you will see a menu on the left-hand edge of the screen headed, "More on [symbol]."

4. Select "Historical Prices," and you will arrive at a page that will allow you to specify the dates for which you want data, and (at the bottom of the page) to download the data into Excel. The table of data you retrieve will include at the right a column of "adjusted close" data, which is adjusted to reflect dividends and share splits.

As with any source of data, accuracy is not guaranteed, so even though we recommend Yahoo Finance as an excellent free research tool, you should protect yourself by confirming the accuracy of the data you download—for example, by calculating calendar year returns using the Yahoo Finance data and comparing those returns to calendar year returns posted on the fund website.

9

The Definitive Portfolio—The Whole Is Greater Than the Sum of Its Parts

Along the way, you have considered alternative solutions to portfolio structure. In this chapter, you will review "The Definitive Portfolio," which consists of two categories of bonds (totaling 25% of your total portfolio), two categories of ETFs (representing domestic stocks, totaling 56.25% of your portfolio), and one category of overseas investment (representing 18.75%) of your capital.

These segments will be invested based upon procedures already discussed, which will be reviewed.

Alternative Portfolio Holdings

You may choose to set aside capital for investment via strategies other than by the construction of the Definitive Portfolio. For example, treasury inflation-protected securities provide such predictable returns that they may be set aside in a separate portfolio of no-risk basic income investments. Bond ladders may be similarly handled.

On the other hand, a diversified buy-and-hold equity-related portfolio may be established for a portion of your investment capital—an excellent strategy for diverse ETFs and/or mutual funds.

If you choose, you may use the Definitive Portfolio as your only investment portfolio or as the portfolio that includes the majority of your investment capital. The amount you may choose to place into such a portfolio (75% of which is in equities) is likely to change with the passage of time and with changing life situations, financial conditions, and investment objectives.

All that said, the Definitive Portfolio provides balance, entry and exit strategies, diversification, risk reduction, and enhanced profit potential. It does have our serious endorsement.

The Four Key Strategies— A Performance Review

You have explored techniques to improve returns with four different types of investments: investment-grade bonds, high yield bonds, domestic equity funds, and international equity funds. Table 9.1 summarizes the historical compounded annual total returns and drawdowns from March 31, 1979 through March 31, 2007. This period includes 28 years of results for the strategies and for buy-and-hold benchmarks against which these strategies may be compared, and is a significant period of study for the purposes.

TABLE 9.1 Four Investment Strategies—Long-Term Performance

Strategy or Benchmark	Annual Compounded Return	Worst Drawdown	Ratio of Annual Return to Drawdown
5-Sector Domestic Equity Rotation	+15.5%	-31%	0.65
International Equity Rotation	+17.9%	-50%	0.36
High Yield Bond Investment Strategy	+ 8.4%[1]	-10%	0.84
Standard & Poor's 500 Index, Buy and Hold	+ 13.0%	-44%	0.30
Lehman Aggregate Bond Index, B & H	+ 8.6%	-13%	0.66

Twenty-Eight Years of Outperformance

Both of the equity-related strategies have produced higher rates of return than buying and holding the Standard & Poor's 500 Index. International funds have proven to have their risks, but their ratio of performance to risk did exceed buy-and-hold strategies for the Standard & Poor's 500 Index, as did the 5-Sector Domestic Equity Rotation Strategy, which produced greater gain with less pain than buying and holding the Standard & Poor's 500 Index. Risk levels associated with international funds have generally been higher than those associated with the Standard & Poor's 500 Index.

The high yield bond-trading strategy provided to high yield bond fund investors annualized rates of return just a bit below those associated with high-quality bonds, with drawdown levels actually below those of the highest grade investment bonds.

Diversifying and Combining to Make the Definitive Portfolio More Profitable Than the Sum of Its Parts

Mission possible: To incorporate these four distinct investment strategies into a comprehensive investment program with the goal of achieving a clearly improved balance between risk and reward. The goal is to improve the balance of reward and risk normally associated with investments in the stock market.

You can accomplish this by first combining the domestic and international equity strategies into one overall equity investment program. Next, you will combine the high yield bond timing strategy and the investment-grade bond benchmark Lehman Aggregate Bond Index in order to formulate an overall fixed-income investment program. And finally, you will combine the overall equity and the overall fixed-income portfolios into the Definitive Portfolio that includes both stocks and bonds.

First Mission Task—Produce Higher Rates of Return at Lower Risk in Your Equity Portfolio

Let's review Table 9.1 once again. You can see that the Domestic Equity Strategy produced average annual gains of 15.5% while showing a maximum drawdown of 31%. The annual gain is nice; the maximum pain is not that great but was less than the 44% maximum loss shown by the Standard & Poor's 500 Index. (This was hardly the worst showing by a market index between 1979–2007. The Nasdaq Composite Index, for example, declined by more than 77% during the 2000–2002 bear market.)

The International Strategy turned up with an annualized rate of return of 17.9% per year (Nice!) but incurred a 50% drawdown (Ouch!) along the way.

What might you expect if you created a portfolio consisting 50% of Domestic Equity Strategy holdings and 50% of International Strategy holdings? The first impulse would be to average the returns (15.5% and 17.9%) and to average the drawdowns (–31% and –50%) for a combined rate of return of 16.7% (halfway between 15.5% and 17.9%) and an average of the two drawdowns (41%, midway between 31% and 50%, rounded to a full number).

Diversification Again Improves Results

As it turns out, the effects of diversification between investments that are not fully correlated once again help the cause. A hypothetical portfolio consisting 50% of the Domestic Equity Strategy and 50% of the International Strategy would have produced an average annual rate of return of 17.1% per year, with a drawdown of 37%—more gain than the average of separate annual rates of return, and less drawdown than the average of the two. (These results assume that the segments were rebalanced at the end of each quarter to start quarterly with equal values.)

Better. Definitely better. The annual rate of return is just fine, at +17.1% per year. However, we do not consider the drawdown of 37% to be acceptable.

Improving Returns by Changing the Portfolio Blend

Inasmuch as the international portion of your stock portfolio mix is more volatile than the U.S. stocks that we are placing into portfolio, the international area may create more risk than we prefer in relationship to the American market.

There are no hard and fast rules that say that all elements within a diverse portfolio have to carry equal weight or be of equal size. Depending upon your risk tolerances or market outlook, you may want to overweight or underweight certain sectors of your portfolio. Given the history of the stock market, we will opt to alter the balance within the Definitive Portfolio so that 75% of its holdings will consist of domestic equity mutual funds or ETFs, and 25% of its holdings will consist of international equity funds or ETFs.

Utilizing the domestic and international equity strategies (see Chapter 4, "Nothing Succeeds Like Success" and Chapter 5, "Worldwide Opportunity") in these proportions would have returned 16.4% per year with a maximum drawdown at any time of 30%. This mix, then, would have returned more each year than the Domestic Equity Strategy alone (which returned 15.5% per annum) at no greater drawdown risk than would be incurred by investing in domestic equities alone.

You Can Eat Better or Sleep Better—The Choice Is Yours

Unfortunately, this is another case of nothing being for nothing. By reducing the relative balance of international-based stockholdings in comparison to the domestic-based stockholdings, we have reduced the historical drawdown from 37% to 30%. That's one for the good guys. However, in the process, we have also reduced the average annual return from 17.1% per year to 16.4%.

At first glance, this seems like a great swap—with your risk reduced by 18.9% and your reward reduced by only 4.1%. However, inasmuch as there are more advancing than declining years for stocks, it is not absolutely clear which would be the more profitable strategy over long periods of time. Because we generally consider the avoidance of loss to be of higher priority than maximizing profit, we suggest the safer course of under-weighting internationals to be the best for most investors.

Figure 9.1 illustrates the recommended allocation of domestic and international equities in the Definitive Portfolio. Figure 9.2 illustrates the compounded rates of return and worst drawdowns for different equity investment programs, 1979–2007. (These represent hypothetical and not real investment returns.)

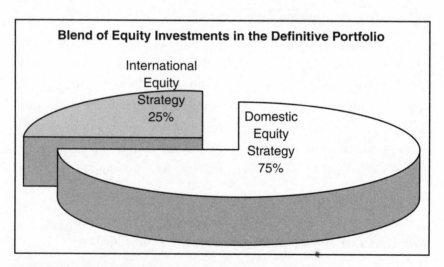

Figure 9.1 Domestic equities represent a larger share of the pie in comparison to international holdings.

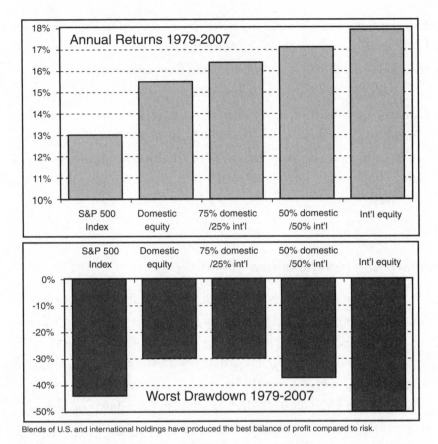

Blends of U.S. and international holdings have produced the best balance of profit compared to risk.

Figure 9.2 Compound gains and worst-case drawdowns for different investment programs.

The Income Component—Preparing a More Profitable Brew from High Yield and Investment-Grade Bonds

As you might expect, a properly diversified ongoing investment portfolio should also include an income component for balance, predictable income flow, and risk reduction.

The Definitive Portfolio will include an income component that, itself, will be diversified with a mix of yield and investment-grade bonds.

In accordance with the general outcomes of diversification, there are likely to be significant benefits from the synergy of these two areas, the mix of which performs better than either area alone.

As you can see, if you review Table 9.1, the high yield strategy that you have learned would have returned 8.4% per year with a 10% drawdown between 1979–2007. A portfolio of high-grade bonds represented by a hypothetical Lehman Aggregate Bond Index Fund would have produced a return of 8.6% per year with a 13% drawdown.

Improving Results with a 50–50 Blend

A portfolio consisting 50% of a hypothetical investment in the Lehman Aggregate Bond Index (a benchmark representing all out-standing investment-grade U.S. bonds) and 50% of a high yield bond portfolio, invested in accordance with the high yield program that you have learned, would have produced returns of 8.6% per year between 1979–2007, with a maximum drawdown of only 8%. Higher returns than the average of the two bond investment approaches; lower drawdown than either alone. Again, we can see the advantages of favorable synergy—the whole greater than the sum of its parts.

Figure 9.3 illustrates the recommended mix of income invest-ments, which consists of 50% investment-grade bonds and 50% high yield bonds. Figure 9.4 illustrates the compounded gains of the indi-vidual components of the income portfolio, and of the combined portfolio for 1979–2007. The results show that a bond portfolio made up of half investment-grade and half high yield bond funds would have been less risky than either type of bond investment alone and, moreover, would have returned as much as the more profitable of the two types of bond investments.

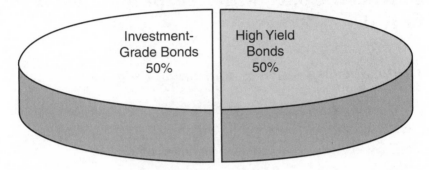

Figure 9.3 Recommended fixed-income program.

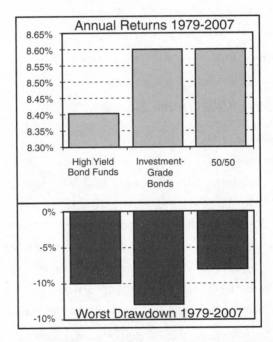

Figure 9.4 Annual compounded returns and drawdowns of the different bond investment programs, 1979–2007.

The Definitive Portfolio of Stocks and Bonds—Returns Sufficient to Meet Your Financial Goals, with Acceptable Levels of Risk

The Final Culmination of Your Study Program

The diversified equity strategy that we have recommended has produced over the 28 years of historical back-testing average annual returns of 16.4% with maximum drawdowns of 30%.

Although these rates of return and risk are superior to the performance of the stock market over the years, risk levels remain too high for our satisfaction. Even risk levels of 20% are likely to prove to be disturbing to most people, although stocks have frequently produced losses in excess of that amount.

The Solution—Blend in the Bonds

The recommended equity strategy (75% domestic and 25% international) returned 16.4% with a drawdown of 30%. The recommended bond strategy (50% high yield and 50% Lehman Aggregate Index Fund) returned 8.6% per year with a maximum drawdown of 8%. If we were to calculate the expected performance of a 50–50 stock/bond portfolio without taking the benefit of diversification into account, we might estimate a historical return of 12.5% per year (halfway between 16.4% and 8.6%) with a worst drawdown of 19% (halfway between the 30% equity drawdown and 8% bond drawdown).

In fact, back testing shows that such a portfolio would have returned 12.8% per year (above our previous estimate), but with a drawdown of only 12%—far lower than the 19% drawdown of our preliminary estimate! Historical returns would have been almost equal to the returns of buying and holding the Standard & Poor's 500

Index (13.0% per year) but with just about only one-fourth the risk of this buy-and-hold (and pray) strategy—(12% versus 44%)!

Improving Returns—If You Can Afford the Risk

The hypothetical past performance shown previously—12.8% return per year on average, coupled with a maximum drawdown level of 12%—presumes that investors have placed 50% of their capital into stocks and 50% into bonds, with both segments invested in accordance with the strategies that we have provided in this work.

This is actually a fairly conservative mix of assets, often suitable for investors near or in retirement for whom capital preservation takes precedence over rates of return. Assets that cannot be replaced do have to be carefully handled, indeed.

Actually, for actively employed investors who can accept somewhat higher levels of risk, a blend of 75% equity-related investments and 25% income-oriented investments is likely to be a mix of choice—a blend of investments that we frequently recommend to clients.

An investment program allocated this way—75% in our favored mix of domestic and international stocks and 25% of assets in a mix of high yield and high grade bonds (instead of the 50–50 blend we introduced before) would have returned 14.7% per year in the hypothetical study, 1979–2007, with a drawdown of 20%. The allocations of this program and its results are illustrated in Figures 9.5 and 9.6.

As you can see, a 75% stock–25% bond mix, as it has been created, clearly outperforms buy-and-hold strategies in both the stock and bond markets at considerably less risk than long-term investments in stocks alone.

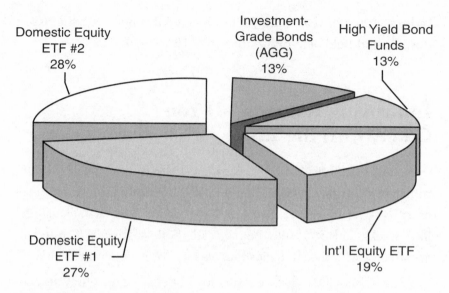

Figure 9.5 Allocations of assets in the 75% stocks–25% bonds Definitive Portfolio.

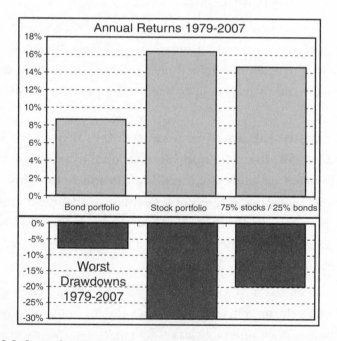

Figure 9.6 Annual returns and worst drawdowns—the bond segment, the stock portfolio, and a mix (75% stocks, 25% bonds). A blend (75% domestic and international stocks, plus 25% bonds) provides an excellent balance between long-term return and risk.

A Final Review of the Steps You Will Need to Take to Achieve Investment Success with the Definitive Portfolio

First, set aside 1/8 of your portfolio assets for placement in investment-grade bonds. For this purpose, we recommend one of the low-expense total bond market index funds such as the iShares Lehman Aggregate Bond ETF (AGG) or the Vanguard Total Bond Market Index Fund (VBMFX).

Second, set aside 1/8 of your portfolio assets for placement in high yield bond funds. Select from high yield bond funds available to you at your brokerage house, emphasizing no-load funds with low expense ratios and fine long-term performance.

Each quarter, evaluate the high yield fund's total return during the previous quarter. This involves calculating the price change in the value of the fund's shares and adding in the total amount that the fund distributed as dividends. This is typically available at the mutual fund's own website.

If the prior calendar quarter's total return of your high yield fund was positive, invest in that fund for the coming quarter. Repeat this procedure each quarter. If your fund made money, maintain your investment for the next quarter. If your high yield fund(s) lost money during a quarter, remove your capital from that fund, re-entering only after it has made money for a quarter.

Stock Components

Third, evaluate the quarterly total returns for each of the ETFs in the following list:

1. iShares S & P 600 Value Index (IJS), which is a small-cap value ETF.

2. iShares S & P 600 Growth Index ETF (IJT), which is a small-cap growth ETF.

3. iShares Russell 1000 Value ETF (IWD), which represents the large-cap value sector.

4. iShares Russell 1000 Growth ETF (IWF), which is a large-cap growth ETF.

5. iShares MSCI EAFE Index ETF (EFA), which is large-cap international.

The two ETFs from this list that gained the most (or lost the least) in the preceding quarter should be in your portfolio for the subsequent quarter. Each of the two ETFs that you select will represent 28.125% of your total portfolio. Repeat your calculations at the end of the quarter. If either of the two ETFs you have selected are no longer first or second in performance, replace it with new leader(s).

Fourth, evaluate the quarterly performance of the three major international ETFs:

1. iShares MSCI Emerging Markets Index (EEM).

2. iShares MSCI Japan Index (EWJ).

3. iShares Europe 350 Index Fund (IEV).

Whichever one of these three had the best returns in the past quarter should be in your portfolio starting the current quarter, representing 18.75% of your capital. Repeat your calculations every quarter. If your ETF has fallen out of the top spot from among the three international ETFs, replace it with the new leader.

Free internet resources that offer you the information you need to carry out these calculations include the following:

1. MSN Money (http://moneycentral.msn.com/investor/charts/charting.asp). This is where you can find ETF and mutual fund share prices for the start and end of every quarter.

2. www.ishares.com. This is the iShares website, where the distribution history for all ETFs used here can be found.

Remember, simply by utilizing low-cost, well-diversified ETFs, including both high yield and investment-grade bonds in your portfolio, and staying on the right side of major market trends simply by following last quarter's winners, you should be able to achieve the capital growth you desire and, in the process, probably outperform most individual and professional investors and market gurus.

10

Don't Let Them Blow You Off the Planet!

Although this book is written for investors of all ages and can benefit anyone, let's look for a moment at readers between fifty to sixty-five years of age. If you happen to be in this age group, the odds are that you are likely to live until at least into your early to mid-80s if medical progress continues along at its present rate.

So far, so good. Haven't longer life spans been a major goal of medical research? Weren't we all pleased when the life span of the average American recently rose to 77.7 years, finally reaching the average life expectancy of the typical European and Canadian, behind whom we had been lagging in longevity?

Senior and near-senior citizens are not only living longer; they are living better, traveling more, still playing golf and tennis, maintaining second homes later into life, continuing to provide financial assistance to children and to grandchildren, taking courses, and otherwise pursuing hobbies, education, fun, and vacations.

Senior citizens have become a major economic engine in the United States and elsewhere, major consumers, and also a major political force. They constitute the most rapidly growing demographic group, particularly among United States residents born within the United States. The Urban Institute, as long ago as 1998, projected to the United States Senate Finance Committee that, between 2010 and 2030, the over-65 population will rise by 70%.

These population trends have already been reflected in the designs of new homes and apartments, in the designs of automobiles, in the activities of travel groups, and in innumerable other ways.

The Bad News

The Urban Institute, which predicted the rise in the over-65 population of 70% by 2030, also projected a rise in the size of the United States labor force through that period—a rise between 2010 and 2030 of just 4%!

Why is this considered bad news? Well, let's take social security, a significant source of income for most retirees, for example. Social security benefits are funded by a national social security trust fund, which receives income from current workers that, along with investment returns to the fund, is theoretically sufficient to provide the assets required to pay out future retirees. And, indeed, the social security program, one of the most popular programs in our national history, has well served the populace since its introduction in 1935. Benefits, which are adjusted for inflation, as well as taxes, have risen over the decades—the original social security tax (1937) was just 2% of payroll per annum. It has since climbed to 12.4% (combined, worker and employer for the first $94,500 income, 2006, due to rise further in the years ahead).

The increased rate of taxation notwithstanding, the entire system appears to be gradually approaching disaster. In 1940, a 65-year-old man might anticipate living for an additional 12.7 years. In 2006, a 65-year-old man had an average additional life expectancy of 15.3 years, an increase of three years (23.6%) of benefit per retiree. Moreover and more significant, in 1965, there were four workers for every social security beneficiary. By 2010, it is anticipated that there will be three. By 2030, it is anticipated that there will be only two workers providing income to the social security trust for every retiree taking benefits. The major pressure on the system lies with the declining percentage of workers and contributors to the social security trust compared to the numbers of people receiving benefits.

Projections of Trouble Time Frames

The Social Security Administration has made the following projections, presuming that current regulations remain in effect.

In 2018, the social security system will begin to pay out more in the way of benefits than it receives in current income from social security taxes. Thereafter, it will have to use the income from securities that it holds (mainly U.S. government bonds) in order to meet its obligations.

By 2028, this income will not be sufficient to meet shortfalls. The system will have to begin to sell securities that it owns as well as use income from retained holdings to meet its obligations.

By 2042, all assets will have been sold. The system will then have enough revenue to pay only 73% of its obligations. Shortfalls will increase thereafter unless either benefits are reduced or new sources of income are located.

Summing Up the Situation

The federal government has already initiated processes of reducing benefits and raising taxes in order to keep the social security program solvent. Initially, the retirement age was set at 65, with an option to take reduced benefits earlier at age 62. The retirement age is presently set at 66 for persons born between 1943 and 1954. It is at 67 for persons born during 1960 or later. The option for reduced benefits at age

62 remains available. Proposals have been made to defer the age of retirement to 70.

Worse Yet?

There are factions in the United States government that would prefer to virtually dissociate the government from social security obligations altogether. Proposals are being made to "privatize" the social security system—to provide means by which beneficiaries can direct the investment of their assets held in the social security trust in various private equity or income investment vehicles, benefits secured from investment proceeds of these investments rather than from government-guaranteed levels of benefits.

In short, if you invest well, you may prosper during retirement. If you invest badly or should the stock and/or bond markets fail to perform during your period of capital accumulation…then what? Well, just don't come knocking on Washington's door.

It looks a little hit or miss. The government may be there to provide for our needs when we all turn old and gray. Or it may not. It might not be a good idea to count on it.

Government Employees May Be No Better Off…

Pressures to remove the guaranteed nature of retirement benefits as a result of potential shortfalls in assets of pension trusts are not limited to the social security system.

Potential shortfalls in funds are likely to occur with committed retirement benefits. For instance, with New York City workers, pension costs, by mid-2006, represented one of the city's fastest-growing expenses, rising from $1.1 billion in 2001 to $4.7 billion by 2006.[1]

Although other estimates are somewhat more sanguine, some projections have suggested that by 2008, New York City pension payouts might well grow to levels where they would represent one dollar of every ten dollars in the city budget.

The situation in New York City is by no means unique. Incipient shortfalls in a number of states, counties, and municipalities have been, to a greater or lesser extent, concealed by use of dubious accounting practices.[2] It is estimated that state and local governments may be obligated to pay benefits to present and future retirees that amount to approximately $375 billion more than they have in current assets.

Fiscal problems are also likely to arise in major cities as a result of promises made by municipal governments to pay not only retirement benefits but also retiree health benefits from trust fund assets originally set aside to meet pension obligations alone.[3] The usual culprits remain operative: underestimation of medical cost inflation, overestimation of income from investments, dubious accounting assumptions, and fear of antagonizing the public or municipal unions.

If trends continue in this direction, there will be little ultimate choice but for governments at all levels to back out of their commitments to meet current pledges of retirement benefits.

Corporations Have Already Begun to Welch on Their Promises...

Private corporations have increasingly been curtailing both retirements and medical benefits to employees and even past retirees who have relied on corporate promises relating to pension benefits. A number of airlines have been particularly egregious in this regard, renegotiating pension benefits after the fact, securing concessions from employees with the threat of declaring bankruptcy.

For example, the number of Fortune 1000 companies that froze or terminated pension plans in 2005 rose by 59 percent to 113.[4] The number of companies closing plans to new hires nearly doubled to 49. Among the well-known companies that have reduced or eliminated guaranteed retirement benefits are Nortel Networks and Verizon.

There have also been reductions in pension plan benefits to employees of companies such as IBM, General Motors, Lockheed Martin, and Motorola.[5] The trend among corporations is to pay out existing pledges of benefits but to fail to offer equal benefit packages to new employees. Guaranteed pension plans have become extremely expensive in part because of lower interest rates in recent years, which have resulted in reduced income to pension trusts that invest in bonds to finance pension plans. This means that employers would have to set aside more money to pay future benefits equal to current payouts to retirees.

As a general rule, newly established retirement plans do not provide guaranteed retirement benefits but are of the 401K variety in which the levels of retirement benefits depend upon the success of employee determined investment selections.

These trends, incidentally, are not limited to the United States by any means. European countries such as Germany, France, and Italy, among others, are encountering difficulties in meeting social guarantees to aging indigenous populations as the ratio of younger workers to the elderly shows relative shrinkage. In Italy, as a matter of fact, the government has been paying bonuses to women who deliver babies.

Japanese births rose for the first time this decade in 2006.[6] The previous year, 2005, had seen an actual shrinkage in the Japanese population of approximately 127 million people, the first on record. The falling birth rate in Japan, as elsewhere, threatens a severe labor shortage and difficulties in paying the health costs and pensions of the elderly in the population.

You probably get the picture by now. Insofar as retirement benefits are concerned, you may not be able to count on the federal government for too many more years. You may not be able to count on local governments for all that many more years as well. And you certainly cannot count on major corporations or other employers for any particular length of time at all.

In the end, you may be able to count only on yourself and your own investing skills.

Rising Medical Expenses, Reduced Medical Cost Protection...

"**Americans worrying about health-care costs.**" *Investment News*, September 25, 2006.

"**...hard times ahead as more employers curtail pension and medical benefits for retirees.**" *Newsday*, June 20, 2006.

"**Medicare costs to increase for wealthier beneficiaries.**" *The New York Times*, September 11, 2006.

If you are like most people, the preceding headlines probably come as no surprise.

Costs of medical care have been among the most rapidly rising of all costs, with annual increases ranging between 10–15%. Health care costs, rising faster than the rest of the economy, have been estimated to amount to approximately 16.6% of the gross domestic product, a very significant expense as well for a large percentage of American families.

As a result of increasing health care expenditures, health insurance plans have been steadily increasing premiums, often at a rate of 8–10% per year. Between 1980 and 1993, spending by employers on health care as a percentage of total compensation to workers rose from 3.3% to 6.6%.[7] This trend has continued since. As a result of rising costs for health benefits, more and more businesses are opting out of or reducing their responsibility for employee health and medical insurance expenses as well as for retiree medical coverage. As a result of the preceding, an increasing percentage of families are finding that rising health expenses—which tend to increase with age in any event—represent a serious and worrisome burden as the years move along.

Medical expenses, unfortunately, frequently force families, already on the financial brink, to turn to their one source of easy, if expensive, money—the credit card—as a last resort at times when their friendly medical insurance carrier refuses to authorize a medically recommended treatment, or when co-pay requirements simply overwhelm their financial resources, or when they are not carrying insurance at all. A report, released in January 2007, indicated that nearly 30% of low- and middle-income families reported using their credit cards to pay medical expenses, often for serious illnesses.[8]

Actually, medical expenses per capita in the United States have been by far the highest in the world, with no particular visible benefit in terms of life spans or general levels of health, in comparisons to countries such as Canada, England, or the Scandinavian nations.

To some extent, these costs represent increasing use of newly developed and expensive medical technology. They also represent inefficiencies in the United States health distribution system such as the various layers of insurance administration, and to some extent higher prices set in the United States for various drugs in comparison to drug pricing overseas. For whatever the reason, costs of medical care and, perhaps, ultimately home or nursing home care, have to be seriously considered in your long-range financial planning. (Approximately 18% of lifetime medical expenses are estimated to be incurred during the last year of life.)

Are They Trying to Blow Us Off the Planet?

Senior citizens no doubt find it interesting in a suspicious sort of way to notice an increasing amount of articles in newspapers and magazines on the subject of whether popular forms of medical treatment are really worth their costs.

Heart bypasses? After countless numbers of such procedures, the medical establishment seems to finally be seriously questioning their cost-effectiveness and value for many patients.

Medicated artery stents? These are also coming into question because of potential stroke risks arising from the use of these as compared to much cheaper unmedicated stents.

Questions are being more frequently raised regarding the necessity of certain medical examinations, blood tests, prostate treatments, mammograms, various surgical procedures, and so forth—with increasing reference to the cost effectiveness of these medical procedures.

In other words, there seems to be an increasing trend to relate potentially life and death medical management decisions to cost and expense. This is not necessarily evil. There may well have been, and perhaps still are, excessive predispositions in both the medical and medical business establishments and among patients for the latest and most sophisticated, if not always necessarily the best and most required, diagnostic tools and treatments. Careful cost re-evaluations were and probably still are inevitable given the aging of the population, the stress of this older population on the medical delivery system, and possibly an inevitable need to ration medical care in one form or another sooner or later.

The social and philosophical implications of whatever form this rationing might take are complex, grave, and potentially unfair in many ways. It has seemed only a brief pause between the celebration of increasing life spans and concern that there may be too many people needing retirement benefits and health services for too long a time for the good of society.

It may be true that in some—perhaps many—cases, more expensive than required medical treatment is proposed to patients by the medical establishment. In other situations, this is definitely not the case. Patients are denied needed medical treatment because of limited finances.

If you are moving into your senior years without ample resources to provide for your own living expenses and for your own medical expenses, you may find that in one way or another, the powers that be may be inclined, actively or by passive neglect, to blow you right off the planet.

Don't let them do that to you.

Your best defense is to become as self-sufficient, economically, as you can and as soon as you can.

According to Saul Friedman, retiring is likely to be boring, lonely, unhealthy, contrary to good sex, and likely to rob your life of meaning and caring except for caring about whether you have enough money left to survive.[9] Mr. Friedman advises workers who are retiring from a job to immediately seek out new employment.

A similar theme was echoed by Liza N. Burby, who expects problems will be created for many retirees by the loss of job identity, the loss of the status created by earned income, and by loneliness resulting from the separation from work companions and business associates.[10]

If the truth be told, post-retirement depressions and problems in adjusting to retirement might, indeed, be the norm—they certainly do occur frequently.

People who own and operate their own closely held businesses seem to be the most reluctant to close shop. They tend to identify with their businesses, to enjoy their work, to remain excited by its challenges, and often end their working lives late and with considerable reluctance. Still, after just a few months of acclimation, these independent operators appear to generally transfer their energies to renewed education, travel, sports if they are still able, physical fitness, concerts—you name it. People with constructive energy during their working years tend to remain interested in life during retirement, only this time with the hours and days available to pursue a broader range of interests.

People who work for other people more often retire quite readily with a sense of relief and to very much enjoy the experience of being masters of their own fate on a daily basis rather than taking orders.

Some professionals—psychoanalysts, for example, and certain other medical specialists—more frequently seem to retire with great reluctance, often quite late in life, with retirement delayed not out of necessity but because of their love of and involvement with their professions.

Back to the other side, for many senior couples, retirement provides opportunities for travel for which there was rarely time prior to retirement, to be with adult children and grandchildren, to pursue new avenues of education, and to be with each other in a way that was not quite possible when life was busier and more externally scheduled.

All of the preceding is simply to say that retirement may be to your liking. It may not. You may want to continue working for as long as you can. You may prefer to be free to do many of the things you have wished for so many years to do. Retirement may take you out of your business loop but it may also provide the time and opportunity to allow you to sample and become involved with many new areas of life.

Wouldn't it really be best if the choice was yours?

When Is the Best Time to Begin to Take Social Security Benefits?

Workers eligible for social security retirement benefits have the option of starting to receive benefits at the age of 62 (early benefits), at ages between 65–67, depending upon their date of birth (full retirement age), or at age 70 (delayed benefits).

Although approximately 60% of retirees elect to take benefits at the age of 62, there are a number of reasons why this might not be the best age to begin, and why it may prove to be better over the long run to elect to defer benefits until at least full retirement age is reached and perhaps later.

Here are some things to consider:

- If you start to take benefits at age 62, your annual benefits will start at and remain between 70–80% (depending on your date of birth) of the benefits of someone who started to take benefits at full retirement age.

If you expect to die relatively early, it would pay to start taking benefits early. If you anticipate a longer life, it would probably pay to wait, if you can afford to.

CAVEAT: If you elect to take early benefits, your benefits would be reduced along the way if you earn a certain amount of money each year. This is not the case if you retire at full retirement age. However, you might, in the latter case, be subject to income tax based upon social security as well as other income.

- If you can afford to wait until 70 to start taking benefits, your benefits, when you do start to take them, may be as much as 130% or so of the benefits that you would receive if you started to take them at full retirement age, depending upon your date of birth. This option is favorable for retirees who do not require immediate income and who expect to live a long life. In addition, social security benefits would not be subject to income taxes

CAVEAT: If you should pass away prior to the age of 70, you would not have received any social security benefits at all, although survivor beneficiaries will.

The total amount of benefits you would receive would become equal at age 77 for the three options: early benefits, benefits starting at full retirement, and benefits delayed until age 70.

CONCLUSION: There is no one decision that is best for all people, though retirement at full retirement age (65–67, depending on date of birth) is probably the best compromise option.

Further Information

Further information regarding the entire social security process, as well as retirement calculators and other data, may be found at a combination of the following websites:

www.socialsecurity.gov: A considerable amount of information may be found at this government site, including calculators of benefits you may expect to receive and relevant regulations.

www.aicpa.org/pubs/jofa.jul2006/garnett.htm: "Social Security: What's the Magic Age?" by Kathryn Garnett.

11

Maybe the Politicians Can't Do It, but You Can—Planning and Carrying Through a Long-Term Financial Program

The political powers appear to be masters at putting off until tomorrow what should be dealt with today. If federal, state, and city pension funds employ dubious accounting assumptions to avoid confrontations with statistical reality, then those dubious accounting assumptions will be accepted by our leaders as reality.

Is this because government leaders at all levels are unaware of the consequences? Or because they are financially inept? Or both? Actually, probably neither of the above.

They simply want to be re-elected. Raising social security taxes today to build up the trust fund for years down the road would be unpopular. So would cutting current benefits, though this has been done indirectly by changes in the tax laws such as the one that made social security payments subject to income taxes and by setting back the age at which full benefits start. Demanding that powerful city unions agree to reduced pension benefits or to reductions in salary to provide ongoing capital for large retirement benefits would, in many cities, be considered political suicide. In New York City, for example, mayors rarely challenge the powerful teacher, police, or firemen unions. Similarly, raising municipal taxes to meet the costs of city worker benefits would probably be political suicide as well. It is definitely easier to sweep the problems under the rug to be dealt with by some future administration.

Flying Today, Paying Tomorrow Has Become the National Pastime...

An airline 30 years ago came up with a marketing campaign for vacationers to fly today and pay tomorrow. It had a snappy ring to it, but was that such a good idea, encouraging people to borrow to take vacations? As life has evolved in the United States (and elsewhere), flying today, paying tomorrow has become the norm rather than the exception. Question: How many of your purchases are paid with cash, by check, or by credit card? If you are like many people, you probably pay cash for only relatively minimum purchases—for food, perhaps, or for subway fares and taxi rides.

Longer trip expenses, restaurant meals, clothes, theatre tickets, significant appliances, jewelry, medical bills—you name it—are probably being paid by credit card, which has also become the coin of the realm for the ever-mounting percentage of purchases made over the Internet.

Credit Cards Feed the Fantasy

There are some good reasons to use credit cards instead of paying by cash, or perhaps to a lesser degree, paying by check.

Credit cards enable people to shop without carrying a lot of cash, which most of us prefer not to do. Leaving large amounts of cash at home is safer, so to that extent, the use of credit cards is reasonable. Credit cards are more convenient than paying by check. Credit card companies provide you with a list of transactions you have made and to some degree maintain your books and records. There are fewer purchases to enter into your check records for balancing. Perhaps convenience is one logical justification for the use of credit cards.

Of more psychological significance perhaps, the use of credit cards provides a sense of magic by encouraging denial of the fact that we will, in the end, have to produce real money that really has to be earned at some point to pay for the purchase that we have just made with a quick signature. The magic of being able to buy at whim just by signing their name on a receipt encourages consumers to deny the actual cost of what they are buying, to minimize the need to think about, to save up for, and to delay expenses for which they might not have cash on hand. For a "mere" 16% or more in interest payments, credit cards provide a feeling of plenty, encouraging impulsive, unnecessary expenditures with only one month-end reckoning.

Take the Quick Credit Card Self-Test

Here's a quick test.

Try to recall a recently made purchase of a not altogether essential but desired item for which you paid by credit card.

Think, if you can, of your state of mind at the time. Would you have made the same purchase if you had to pay by writing out a check?

Would you have made the same purchase if you had to pay with actual, real, green dollars—counting out bill by bill the amount that you were spending? Would the purchase have seemed more expensive if you had paid by cash?

Would almost all purchases seem more expensive if you were to pay by cash?

Would you have left the same tip at your last restaurant meal if you had left the tip in cash on the table rather than as a credit card addendum to the restaurant bill? (Restaurants rarely ask any more for tips to be left on the table.)

In how many ways, how many times, in making a choice of a credit card purchase, do you choose a more-expensive rather than less-expensive option? Would you make the same choices if you were paying by cash rather than by credit card?

Businesses know the answers—which is why it is a rare business indeed, nowadays, that does not have a credit card machine at the handy ready.

Instant Money-Saving Idea

I'm sure you've guessed it. **Simply, pay with cash, not by credit card,** wherever and whenever possible. See how much more frequently you re-evaluate your purchases before buying. See how much more your shopping is controlled. See how much money you actually save by reducing impulse buying.

See how much you can save in interest by deferring purchases until you actually can pay cash for them. Credit card interest charges do add considerably to costs of living, by promoting impulse buying and by promoting the use of high-cost credit to do so. Is it really worth it to pay 16%–20% (plus late charges) more for what you buy just to buy sooner?

Second Instant Money-Saving Idea

At the time that you consider the purchase of something, simply ask yourself how many hours did you or will you have to work to earn the money required for the acquisition.

The answers will vary, of course, with your income level. Some people have high incomes—really high incomes. Between these incomes and possibly accumulated assets, there may be only relatively minimal restrictions on what they can afford to spend, in addition to which they have the ability to pay credit card bills immediately, thereby avoiding interest charges. Most people, however, may find that the question will actually make them reconsider purchases when the price is measured not just in money but also in the expenditure of actual labor to earn that money.

For example, you want a new designer sweater, which costs $400 after-tax money. You make $52,000 per year, about $1,000 a week before taxes. You will have to work just about three days to earn the $600 pre-tax dollars that the sweater, at a price of $400, will cost in after-tax dollars. Three days of riding the subway or bus or driving in the rush hour, three days of dealing with your boss, and three days of handling customers, clients, or computer. Think about it. Do you really still need or still want that sweater?

Extending the Concept of Paying by Cash to Accumulate the Assets You Will Need Throughout Life

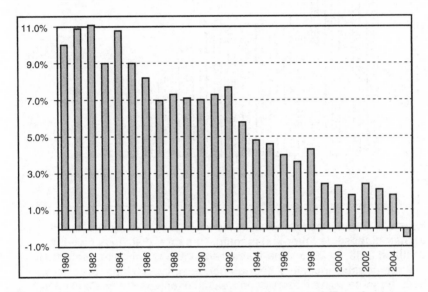

Figure 11.1 Can you guess what this figure represents? Turn the page for the answer.

Some of us are fortunate enough to earn sufficient money from our jobs, businesses, or, perhaps, inherited wealth and assets, to be able to afford almost any conceivable desire without having to calculate its cost in terms of labor required or to have to consider less-expensive alternative purchases.

Most families or people, however, are not quite that fortunate and do have to make choices—purchase this or do that, buy now or wait until later, expand the house or take a vacation, send children to state schools to save on tuition costs or seek out a private university, spend the higher amount or reserve something for your saving and accumulation program. As you shall see, the earlier you start, the more readily you can accumulate the assets required during your later years, as well as assets that may be needed to pay for more current family expenses such as your children's education.

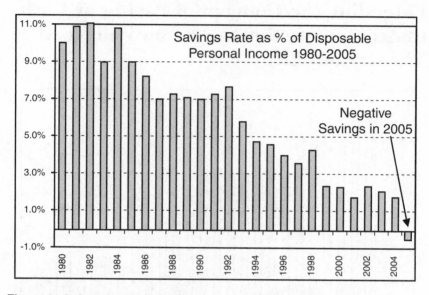

Figure 11.2 American families, in the early 1980s, saved up to 11% of their disposable (after-tax) income. This rate of savings steadily declined until, by 2005, Americans were actually spending more than their disposable income. Although decreases in savings rates have been offset to some degree by increases in assets set aside in 401K and similar retirement plans, and by increases in the value of people's homes, the tendency of Americans to spend to the hilt has become strikingly alarming.

In years past, certainly in the years following the great depression of the 1930s, it was more the general practice of American families to first save a certain portion of income each week and then to live off the remainder. As the decades have passed, and as the depression has become more and more only a dim cultural recollection, a national emphasis on saving has given way to a psychology of consumption— the process supported by the forces of advertising that surround us and our children, by social competitiveness, and by an extension of the credit card psychology to a general national psychology of more or less instant gratification.

Shopping has become a major national pastime in the United States—buying a significant form of weekend entertainment for many families, the shopping mall a far more likely weekend destination than a local nature preserve or museum.

If you are like most people, a program of saving for future needs, of avoiding, to the best of your ability, unnecessary debt, and of involving your entire family in this process, may seem unnatural and even cruel. However, it is not cruel—not at all. If you, as a parent or parents, can help your children learn to prioritize their wishes and to defer gratification if need be, and if you can help yourself in that same manner, you will have rendered a service to your entire family, indeed.

Once again, the earlier you start to accumulate cash for the future, the more steadily you can follow an accumulation program, and the more you will acquire for needs that present themselves later in life.

How Much Money Will You Need for Retirement Purposes?

You have worked hard for many years. You have provided for your children and for others who may have needed your help. You have been able to achieve a comfortable lifestyle that you would like to maintain into retirement. You are looking forward to doing some of those things, to seeing some of those places that you have not been able to do or to see because of life's work and financial obligations. In short, your turn is coming. How much will you need in assets to live as you hope?

The Magic Twenty!

Well, let's suppose that to maintain your present lifestyle during retirement, you would require $150,000 in pre-tax income, about 75–80% of your expenses while you were working (a general, possibly optimistic assumption). You would like to know that, pretty much come what may, you can count on this amount of income flow.

There have been very few periods over the past several decades during which it has not been possible to secure income from virtually risk-free investments of at least 5% of the amount of capital invested. For example, presently, 90-day treasury bills, the safest of all investments, are paying income to investors at a rate of approximately 5% per annum. High-quality municipal bonds, tax exempt, carrying minimal risk, and paying virtually the same rate of interest as U.S. treasury bills, are available as well.

If you were to invest in such instruments, which paid 5%, or 1/20 of your investment assets, per annum, you would require an asset base of twenty times your annual expenses to produce a virtual guarantee of the income required to maintain your desired lifestyle.

Calculation

First, we will assume that you are receiving $25,000 per year in social security benefits, which can be deducted from the $150,000 pre-tax annual income you expect to need. You will, therefore, require an additional $125,000 in investment income to achieve a total pre-tax income of $150,000.

Twenty times $125,000 would equal $2,500,000. If you manage to accumulate $2,500,000 and secure an investment rate of return of 5% per annum (which would come to $125,000) on this amount of assets in addition to $25,000 social security, you would be assured of your required income of $150,000. Your requirements for $150,000 per year would be easily met with safe and simple investments, which is why we refer to this as the "Magic Twenty"—twenty times the amount of income flow you will require from your investments.

Adjustments That May Be Required

The preceding calculation makes some assumptions. First, we are presuming that you never want to see any reduction in the amount of your assets, even while you are aging and living off their proceeds. Second, we are not including the value of assets such as your home— we are presuming cash assets only. Many elderly people do sell larger homes as they age, moving to smaller quarters—a process likely to increase their cash positions.

Making the Adjustment for Inflation

If we were to presume a 2.5% per year rate of inflation, which would reduce your buying power by 2.5% per year unless you increased your income accordingly, an annual rate of return on your investments of 5% would be insufficient to maintain your lifestyle as well as your total capital base over a very protracted period of time. You would have to either strive for a higher rate of return from your investments, perhaps to 7.5% per year (5% plus 2.5% inflation adjustment) or start with a greater amount, forty times your initial annual expenses rather than twenty times.

Let's work this out. You require at the start $125,000 per year in income after you receive your social security benefits (which are adjusted for inflation). If you are securing a 5% inflation unadjusted rate of return, the value of this return must be adjusted downwards by 2.5% per year to reflect loss of buying power, leaving a net, inflation-adjusted return, of 2.5% (5% annual income—2½% loss of buying power). If we divide the desired total return ($125,000) by .025 (2.5%), we secure the amount of capital needed to produce $125,000 at a rate of return of 2.5%. This comes to $5,000,000 ($125,000 desired income divided by .025 = $5,000,000) or forty times the amount of income desired.

So, let's think of two magic numbers, which presume basic rates of inflation over the years to lie in the area of 2.5%:

> **The Magic Twenty**—The multiple of your assumed retirement expenses required to maintain your lifestyle, unadjusted for inflation, assuming a rate of return from your investments of 5% per year.
>
> **The Fabulous Forty**—The multiple of your assumed annual retirement expenses required to maintain your lifestyle, adjusted for $2\frac{1}{2}$% annual inflation, assuming a rate of investment returns of 5% per year from your assets.

Neither goal is necessarily easy to attain, so most retirees are likely to find themselves in positions in which they must take some risk for higher returns, reduce their lifestyle goals, continue to maintain employment at some level, and/or incur some level of drawdown of their assets as the years pass.

Obviously, the closer you can achieve the accumulation of assets at or close to the "magic numbers," the better. The presumed rate of investment return of 5% that we have been employing is probably a rather conservative target. For example, over the long run, stocks have tended to produce rates of return in the order of 10% per year that, if achieved, would provide for your needs even if you started with considerably less in initial assets.

Table 11.1 shows the impact of even a moderate rate of inflation, 2.5% per annum, on the buying power of an amount of capital over a twenty-year period. With life expectancies increasing and living costs such as medical expenses rising, it is becoming more imperative than ever to accumulate sufficient assets to maintain a viable lifestyle for the years following retirement.

TABLE 11.1 Loss of Buying Power at 2.5% Rate of Inflation

Year	Starting Amount	Buying Power
1	100,000	100,000
2	100,000	97,500
3	100,000	95,063
4	100,000	92,686
5	100,000	90,369
6	100,000	88,110
7	100,000	85,907
8	100,000	83,759
9	100,000	81,665
10	100,000	79,624
15	100,000	70,156
20	100,000	61,814

Commentary

The present-day value of $100,000 will become reduced to $79,624 in 10 years and to $61,814 in 20 years. Retirement planning should include recognition of the likely loss of buying power over the years.

The message is clear! Start early! Accumulate consistently! Stay with the plan!

Make no mistake about it. This will not be easy. You will be fighting advertising campaigns that take aim right at your subconscious—subliminal placements of products in movie scenes, James Bond wearing Omega watches, teenage idols wearing clothes your children will request, nifty cars for women to admire—automobiles are generally sold to men, not to women.

You may well be fighting your own life conditioning to buy when the impulse strikes, the ready availability of credit cards. Credit card companies have even been offering credit cards to children in high school and to college-age young adults who have no independent source of income.

You may well be fighting subtle and not-so-subtle promises by the government that things will be better in the years ahead, that your stocks will keep soaring, and that home values will rise forever.

And you may well be fighting images of your neighbors renovating your entire block while you still worry about the heating bills. They may or may not be fixing up on credit, but after all, you still do not want to live in the smallest house in the area.

The earlier you start, the better. The more consistently you add to your basic accumulation assets, the better. The more consistently you can make your assets grow while avoiding serious loss, the better.

Let's review some alternative investment plans.

Examples of Asset Growth—Relatively Modest Rate of Growth of Relatively Moderate Capital Base, with Relatively Moderate Annual Additions to Your Assets

(We recognize that for a large proportion of families, the amounts of assets that are employed in the following examples are hardly moderate, and that there are periods when the achievement of the rates of return we are assuming cannot be readily accomplished.)

Figure 11.3 illustrates the growth of capital over periods of up to 25 years employing the following assumptions:

1. Your assets start with $200,000. You make no additional contributions and all profits remain within the plan to compound at a rate of 8% per year, our assumed rate of capital growth.

2. Your assets start with $200,000, but in this case you add $10,000 per year each year to your asset base, so your holdings increase because of an 8% presumed growth rate and because you are augmenting the assets in the account each year in addition to fully re-investing profits.

3. You have no assets to start, but add $10,000 each year, left in the program to compound at 8% per year.

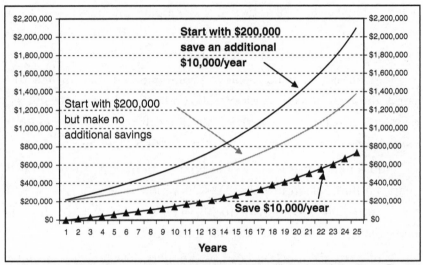

Figure 11.3 shows the growth of assets over 25 years based upon three different accumulation patterns. The most productive pattern, in which an investor starts with $200,000, adds $10,000 per year, and earns 8% per year on his capital, would result in asset deposits totaling $450,000, growing to more than $2.1 million in 25 years.

Figure 11.3 Compound growth of assets invested at 8% per year.

You may notice the annual acceleration of growth over the years as capital compounds for longer periods of time. An initial deposit of $200,000 gains only a little more than $17,000 in its second year of investment but gains more than $100,000 in its twenty-fifth year. The more you invest, and the longer the investment period, the more accelerated is the growth of your capital.

The Effects of Higher Rates of Return Are Considerable

An initial investment of $200,000, not augmented over the years, but allowed to grow without withdrawals, would grow to $1,369,695 in 25 years, presuming a rate of return of 8% per annum. Actually, a good case can be made for expectations of higher rates of return based upon normal long-term rates of return from the stock market (approximately 10% per annum) and our belief that you are likely to achieve higher rates of return if you employ the investment techniques discussed in this book. Neither can be guaranteed, but we, nonetheless, believe that the goals implied are realistic.

Presuming that you do achieve a compound rate of return of 10% per annum, an initial deposit of $200,000 would grow to $2,166,941 over a 25 year period, or to $797,246 more than the same amount of capital showing a compound rate of return of 8% per year.

Add another five years to the holding period. At the end of 30 years, an initial deposit of $200,000, compounding at a rate of 10% per year, would have grown to $3,489,880! This would represent more than a 17-fold growth of your initial investment.

While we are thinking positive thoughts, let's imagine an initial deposit of $200,000 growing at a rate of 12% per year for a period of 30 years. How would a final tally of $5,991,984 sound? This amount would be able to provide an annual income of more than $299,500 if you then invested for an absolutely safe return of just 5% per year.

Even Smaller Asset Bases Can Add Up Over the Years if You Stay Consistent...

For example, let's suppose that you started with no capital, but added $10,000 per year for 25 years and that your assets grew at a moderate 8% per year. You would still end up with $731,059, nearly triple your invested capital over the years. Not enough, perhaps, to live the retirement life of your dreams, but enough to provide $36,553 in annual income at investment returns of just 5% per year. If you were to maintain an 8% annual growth rate, your annual income from investment capital would come to $58,485.

Starting Earlier in Life Can Make a Substantial Difference in the Growth of Your Assets

The compounding effects of investment become more and more significant the earlier you start your investment program. For example, Figure 11.4 compares the results of carrying forth a 30-year program of asset accumulation in comparison to carrying forth only a 10-year accumulation program that, however, started 10 years earlier in life, maintaining both accounts until the same ending time.

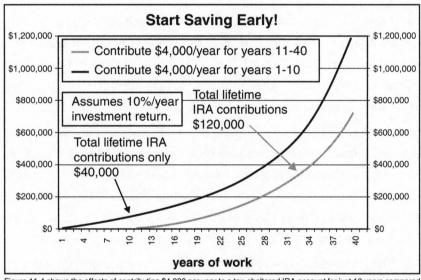

Figure 11.4 shows the effects of contributing $4,000 per year to a tax-sheltered IRA account for just 10 years compared to contributing $4,000 per year for 30 years, if both are held to the same point in time, 40 years from the end of the first 10-year period of contributions, and 30 years from the start of the second, this time 30-year, period of contributions.

Figure 11.4 The power of long-term compound returns.

The Power of Compounding

Would you like to really give a child a gift of growth?

It is possible to establish an IRA account for children that will allow you to match up to $4,000 of income that they have earned with the creation of an IRA that would allow your contributions to grow tax-free until your children take distributions at some point in the distant future.

Let's suppose that you establish such an IRA at a time that your child is 20 years old, working part-time and earning at least $4,000 per year. For 10 years, until the child is 30, you deposit $4,000 annually in an IRA, making no further contributions thereafter. We will assume that investments under the umbrella of this IRA grow at a rate of 10% per year. How much would that initial $40,000 (10 years × $4,000) grow to at the end of 40 years, or at the time your child is 60 years of age?

Figure 11.4 tells the story. That initial $40,000 would grow to $1,223,633, or to more than 30.5 times the amount of assets you placed into the IRA account! This is virtually a retirement asset base in and of itself, which would grow to nearly $2 million by the time your child reaches the age of 65.

As an alternative, let's suppose that your child had an IRA that he started to fund at age 30, into which he placed $4,000 per year starting at age 30, maintaining this amount as an annual investment until age 60, a 30-year process that involved a final total of $120,000 in contributions, rather than the $40,000 in the previous program. What would be the growth of this $120,000 over the coming 30 years?

The IRA, when your child reaches 60, at a compound growth rate of 10%, would grow to $723,773, or to just 6.03 times the amount of contributions that had been placed into the program.

For the 30-year period, annual contributions totaling $120,000 grow to just $723,773. Not bad, not bad at all, but not as positive appearing compared to the 40-year period of time, during which only $40,000 placed into the program grows to $1,223,633, 30.5 times the assets contributed.

Table 11.2 shows the comparative growth of these two investing options.

TABLE 11.2 Forty Years of Capital Growth
Capital Earns 10% Per Annum During Each of the Forty Years

Year	Invest $4,000 During Each Ten Years, Nothing Thereafter	Invest $4,000 Between Years 11–40
1	4,400	
2	9,240	
3	14,564	
4	20,420	
5	26,862	
6	33,949	
7	41,744	
8	50,318	
9	59,750	
10	70,125	
11	77,137	4,400
12	84,851	9,240
13	93,336	14,564
14	102,670	20,420
15	112,936	26,862
16	124,230	33,949
17	136,653	41,744
18	150,318	50,318
19	165,350	59,750
20	181,885	70,124
21	200,074	81,537
22	220,081	94,091
23	242,089	107,900
24	266,298	123,090
25	292,928	158,179
27	354,443	178,397
28	389,887	200,636
29	428,876	225,100
30	471,764	52,010
31	518,940	81,611
32	570,834	314,172
33	627,917	349,989
34	690,709	389,388
35	759,780	432,727

TABLE 11.2 Continued

Year	Invest $4,000 During Each Ten Years, Nothing Thereafter	Invest $4,000 Between Years 11–40
36	835,758	480,400
37	919,334	532,840
38	1,011,268	590,524
39	1,112,394	653,976
40	1,223,634	723,774

The ability of the first option (investing ten years sooner) to maintain its lead over the second option in spite of the additional contributions involved over the 30-year period compared to the 10-year period is quite striking and well illustrates the concept that the earlier you start to accumulate capital, by far the better.

One Final Example of the Power of Compounding—The One Contribution Retirement Fund

Figure 11.5 shows the effects of making just a one-time contribution to a retirement program relatively early in your working life, and allowing that contribution to grow and to compound for 40 years as part of your tax-sheltered retirement fund.

Figure 11.5 is probably self-explanatory.

Let's suppose that you are a successful young professional, or have hit a bonus jackpot on Wall Street, or in some other manner have managed, by the time you are 20 to 30 years of age, to have accumulated $40,000 that you can place into a tax shelter of some form—perhaps a 401K plan, perhaps a tax-sheltered variable annuity, or perhaps an IRA that your parents gifted to you along the way.

This amount of $40,000 is placed into a retirement fund, never augmented, but allowed to grow at a rate of 10% per year for 40 years. What would be its ending value at that time?

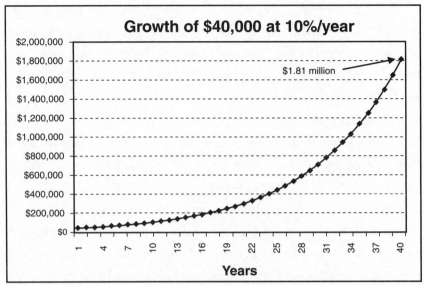

$40,000, deposited into a tax-sheltered account, and allowed to compound at 10% per year, will grow over a 40-year period to more than $1.8 million—perhaps a retirement base in and of itself.

Figure 11.5 Compounding a single contribution for forty years.

That original deposit of $40,000 will grow to more than $1.8 million, or to more than 45 times the initial deposit!

The moral: Even if life expenses rise with the growth of your family, with the purchase of your home, with whatever—if you can get your retirement fund up early, you can still accumulate sufficient capital to meet your needs later in life.

We are sure that you get the idea by now. Sooner is better. Much sooner is much better. You will not necessarily have to fund your retirement program with great sums of money if you start early and contribute regularly.

Summing Up

Most Americans are not saving nearly enough for the future, and are likely to find themselves in deep financial trouble as the years move along, particularly if current trends in pension financing and increases in medical costs continue.

You can dig in and combat these trends in your own lives by committing yourself to savings and investment plans designed to maintain your lifestyle as your life moves along. The more expensive your lifestyle, the more assets you will need to place into your accumulation fund.

The earlier you start your accumulation process, the longer you can allow your assets to grow, the larger the amounts you will have available at those times when you will have to draw from your investment plan for living and other expenses.

You have seen something of why the government cannot be counted on to provide for our security. You have seen something of what you want to achieve. Perhaps by now you have arrived at some estimate of what your financial goals will have to be to achieve the lifestyle and security that you and your family desire.

Appendix

Internet Resources for Investors

ETF Websites

www.etfconnect.com

This site contains useful information about the performance, expense ratios, and composition of ETFs and closed-end mutual funds. Historical price data can be exported easily into Excel files. For investors who want to study SEC filings (such as annual shareholder reports or financial statements) of particular ETFs or closed-end funds, www.etfconnect has links to the SEC website that are much easier to use than attempting to navigate www.sec.gov directly.

http://finance.yahoo.com

From this homepage, look to the lower left to find the list of links under "Investing." The link to ETFs will take you to "ETF Center." There is a menu of options in the ETF center, including the ability to rank ETFs by performance, trading volume, assets, and so on. This website also provides more detailed information about the holdings in some individual ETFs including sector exposures and valuation measures.

www.xtf.com

From the homepage of the XTF website, select one of the "research tools and resources" links, and from there, select "ETF Rating Service."

Enter the ticker symbol of the ETF you want to research. This website provides bid-ask spreads, earnings yields, and dividend yields—data that can sometimes be difficult to obtain accurately. Other information available on xtf.com is average daily volume, expense ratio, underlying benchmark index, top holdings, and sector breakdown. The site also provides more subjective comments such as the amount of liquidity and the attractiveness as an investment. We have not attempted to evaluate the validity of any judgments that XTF has posted on its website.

www.ishares.com

We consider this the best ETF sponsor website, which contains information about the largest family of ETFs, iShares.

Historical and Current Mutual Fund, ETF, and Stock Performance Data

http://moneycentral.msn.com/investor/charts/charting.asp

This website provides a simple and very useful tool for charting, which can quickly give you a visual overview of an investment's history. You can compare the performance of different investments on the same chart, and you can specify the period displayed. If there is a particular part of the chart for which you want numerical data, you can point your cursor to it or you can download the price history (for just one investment) from the chart into Excel.

There is a menu of hyperlinks on the left part of the screen that allows you to jump to a quote page. For individual stocks, the quotes are delayed (and are therefore not useful for trading), but the quote page contains other useful information such as dividend amount and yield, earnings/share, and market capitalization.

http://finance.yahoo.com

This website is an excellent resource for historical mutual fund, ETF, and index pricing data. On the homepage, enter the ticker symbol of the ETF or mutual fund for which you want historical total return data. Doing so will get you to a new screen with the latest intra-day quote (delayed). On the left of this screen, click on the link to historical data.

The historical data screen has open, high, low, and closing price data, as well as "adjusted close" data. Adjusted close data reflects total returns: dividend payments and splits for stocks, distributions for mutual funds, and ETFs. At the bottom of the page is a link that will allow you to download the historical data to an Excel spreadsheet.

Most sources of total return data on mutual funds miss some distributions. The further back in history you go, the more likely you are to encounter some error in the data. We have found Yahoo Finance data to be reasonably accurate, but as with any free data source, you should if possible verify the accuracy of distribution and total return histories.

Historical Economic Data

http://www.federalreserve.gov/releases/H15/data.htm

The historical interest rate data used in the book came from the Federal Reserve statistical release H.15 "Selected Interest Rates," available at the preceding URL.

www.irrationalexuberance.com

Professor Robert Shiller at Yale released the first edition of his book, *Irrational Exuberance*, in a timely manner shortly before the stock market peaked in March 2000. This website contains historical stock market price, dividend, and earnings data, as well as inflation and housing price data that you can download for free in Excel format.

Endnotes

Chapter 1

1. Within a number of chapters, incidentally including this one, there will be special side articles, derived from studies by Dr. Marvin Appel, which have appeared in "Systems & Forecasts," a stock market newsletter founded by Gerald Appel in 1973, of which Marvin is the current editor. These articles present relatively little-known insights into tools and techniques that may be employed for market forecasting. We believe that they represent a special and unique feature in this work.

2. By Marvin Appel, Ph.D., extracted from "Systems & Forecasts." February 17, 2006.

Chapter 2

1. For a very useful and special strategy for the selection of mutual funds leading in performance, we refer readers to *Opportunity Investing*, by Gerald Appel (Prentice Hall 2007).

2. Readers may refer to *Opportunity Investing*, cited previously, or to the Internet via a search for "closed-end mutual funds."

3. Information can be secured from Morningstar reports, and from financial statements issued by funds themselves.

4. Readers who would like to acquire more detailed knowledge of ETFs and additional investment strategies with these instruments may want to secure a copy of *Trading in Exchange Traded Funds Made Easy*, by Marvin Appel (Prentice Hall 2007). Fuller

descriptions of the book, reviewer comments, and ordering procedures can be found at Amazon.com.

Chapter 3

1. The *Quotable Investor*, Sanford Jacobs, editor. Lyons Press (Guilford, CT), 2001, page 120.

2. The Standard and Poor's Homebuilding Index is tracked by an ETF with ticker symbol XHB.

3. It is unfortunately not true that every index fund is low cost. For example, there are a number of relatively expensive S&P 500 Index funds sold by full-service/full-price brokers. You should limit your index fund investments to those offered by Vanguard, Fidelity, or similarly inexpensive offerings (including ETFs) that may be available to you in particular retirement plans.

4. See, for example, the section titled "Frequent Trading Limits" in the prospectus dated August 17, 2006 to the Vanguard 500 Index Fund.

5. When determining how much weight a stock will have in an index such as the S&P 500, most index providers exclude from consideration "closely held" shares such as those owned by the founding family that are unlikely ever to be for sale. The market capitalization excluding closely held shares is called the *free float*.

6. *Stocks, Bonds, Bills and Inflation 2005 Yearbook*, Ibbotson Associates (Chicago), 2005.

7. Risk is calculated in stocks, bonds, bills, and inflation as the standard deviation of annual returns. The standard deviation for large stocks, 19.15%/year, is normalized to 1.0. All other risks are reported in Table 3.2 as multiples of the risk for large-cap stocks.

8. Source: *Stocks, Bonds, Bills and Inflation 2005 Yearbook*, Ibbotson Associates (Chicago), 2005.

9. As in Table 3.2, risk is again calculated as the standard deviation of annual returns, normalized so that the risk of large-cap stocks during the period is set to 1.0, and other risks are reported as multiples of the risks of large-cap stocks. During the 1969–2004 period, the annualized standard deviation of large-cap stock returns was 17.8%. Because this is slightly lower than the level of volatility (19.15%) calculated for the same group of stocks over a longer period (1926–2004), the implication is that stocks have been safer since 1969 than they were before 1969.

10. For completeness, it should be noted that in addition to the $400 billion in equity REITs, there is another $40 billion in REITs that function as mortgage lenders. We will not consider such mortgage REITs. Source: www.nareit.com.

Chapter 4

1. Growth managers have in general fared better against their index benchmarks than have value or blend managers. As an example, Table 4.1 shows the performance of the large-cap growth ETF (IVW) merely matched but did not beat that of the median large-cap growth mutual fund from 1997–2007.

2. On orders to buy or sell at least 500 shares under normal mid-day market conditions, March 22, 2007.

3. This is the percentage of actively managed mutual funds that the benchmark index outperformed during the March 1997–Feb. 2007 (120 months) period when both risk and returns were taken into account. (The specific performance measure is called the Sharpe Ratio.) The higher the percentage, the greater the performance of the benchmark relative to actively managed

funds. None of these ETFs has been around for the full 10 years, so in order to formulate a reasonable comparison, results of the underlying benchmark minus the ETF expense ratio are stacked up against the universe of mutual funds in operation at least 10 years. Source: Mutual Fund Expert database of 2/28/2007.

4. Data on the two Russell indexes (large-cap value and small-cap value) goes back to 1979, and data on the EAFE index (international) is available all the way back to 1970, but the S&P indexes (large-cap growth and small-cap growth) began only in 1996. In order to generate the hypothetical historical performance data shown in Figure 4.2, Russell large-cap and small-cap growth indexes were used in the study from 1979 until the better-performing S&P indexes became available. Even if you had limited yourself to using only Russell indexes throughout the entire 1979–2007 period, the asset allocation strategy would have outperformed each of the indexes individually.

5. Paraphrase of a quote by Warren Buffett regarding hedge funds in *Dean LeBaron, Romesh Vaitilingam, and Marilyn Pitchford, Dean LeBaron's Book of Investment Quotations*. Wiley, 2002 (New York), page 136.

6. The average drawdown of the 366 funds studied was 44.1%, yet when these 366 funds were combined as a highly diversified portfolio, the drawdown shrank to 35.6%, as reported in the table. The implication is that diversification, as would be expected, reduced risk.

Chapter 5

1. Source: iShares website information on the MSCI Emerging Market Index ETF, ticker symbol EEM, on 5/9/2007. (http://www.ishares.com/fund_info/detail.jhtml;jsessionid=ZGHS0MN HGU3IERJUMTCBBGSFGQ0EOD50?symbol=EEM)

2. If you count the oil theoretically recoverable from its tar sands, Canada's energy reserves would exceed those of every other country except Venezuela and Saudi Arabia, according to Rigzone.com, an oil industry website. (http://www.rigzone.com/news/article.asp?a_id=30703)

3. http://www.investaustralia.gov.au/media/FLAGSHIP_final English.pdf

4. DWS Global Thematic Fund semi-annual report (2/28/2007).

5. These performance figures are based on the monthly total returns not including taxes or transaction costs of the MSCI Europe and U.S. Market Indexes. Source: http://www.mscibarra.com/products/indices/stdindex/performance.jsp.

6. Data are based on the quarterly total returns of the MSCI Europe, MSCI Far East, and MSCI Emerging Markets Indexes in U.S. dollars without counting taxes or transaction costs.

7. These figures are arrived at by comparing the returns on the MSCI "Gross" Indexes, which do not take withholding into account, and the corresponding MSCI "Net" Indexes," which do.

Chapter 6

1. LeBaron, Dean, Vaitilingam, Romesh, and Pitchford, Marilyn. *Dean LeBaron's Book* of *Investment Quotations*. Wiley, 2002.

2. Yield-to-maturity of underlying bonds less the ETF expense ratio. Source: www.ishares.com on April 17, 2007.

Chapter 7

1. The compounded annual return of the Lehman Aggregate Bond Index from 1982–2007 was 9.3%/year.

2. Source: Standard and Poor's (http://www.riskglossary.com, search under "default model").

3. Source: Fitch Ratings. "The Shrinking Default Rate and the Credit Cycle—New Twists, New Risks," Feb. 20, 2007. (http://www.fitchratings.com/corporate/reports/report_frame.cfm?rpt_id=314628).

4. Estimated by taking the yield on the Merrill Lynch High Yield Bond Index, Constrained, as reported in the *Wall Street Journal* on 2/6/2007, and subtracting the typical 1% expense ratio of high yield bond mutual funds.

5. Different share classes of the same fund are counted as one distinct fund.

6. https://www.oppenheimerfunds.com/pdf/prospectuses/srfloatingratefund.pdf, prospectus dated 9/27/2006.

7. HFLIX is the institutional class share, which is the Hartford Floating Rate Fund share type that pays the highest dividend. It is available without a front-end sales charge to individual investors at T.D. Ameritrade. Customers at Schwab can buy the A-class share, ticker HFLAX, also without paying the usual 3% front-end sales charge. The A-class share pays a lower dividend than the institutional class share. You should in no circumstances pay a front-end or deferred sales charge to buy this or any other mutual fund, and you should check with your discount brokerage house to see which is the highest-yielding, lowest-expense class of shares available to you.

8. Specifically, the increase in the Consumer Price Index for Urban Consumers as calculated by the Bureau of Labor Statistics.

9. A subset of municipal bonds, called private activity bonds, is subject to the alternative minimum tax (AMT). You should ascertain before investing in municipal bonds whether or not the interest will be taxable for AMT purposes, and whether or not that is likely to affect you.

10. As reported on www.vanguard.com on 4/3/2007.

11. The website www.investinginbonds.com has a section, "Municipal market at a glance," in which you can view all municipal bond transactions by date. You can draw inferences on broker mark-ups from transactions marked "sale to customer" that occurred immediately following an inter-dealer transaction for the exact same bonds.

Chapter 8

1. www.fitchratings.com. "The Shrinking Default Rate and the Credit Cycle—New Trists, New Risks," Feb. 20, 2007, page 1.

2. *Ibid.*

3. The URL for Yahoo Finance is http://finance.yahoo.com. For instructions on how to download total return data from this site, please see the Appendix to this chapter.

4. Northeast Investors does not have an affiliated money market, so transactions with that fund company must be handled through the mail. This can be cumbersome, but you can avoid the hassle if you buy Northeast Investors Trust through a discount brokerage mutual fund platform such as Schwab's or T.D. Ameritrade's.

5. http://www.brainyquote.com/quotes/authors/y/yogi_berra.html.

6. Merrill Lynch High Yield Bond 100 Index yield as reported in the *Wall Street Journal* of March 13, 2007.

7. Ned Davis Research, chart B334, monthly data through 3/31/2007.

8. Ned Davis Research, chart B0334, monthly data through 2/28/2007.

Chapter 9

[1.] The 8.4% annual gain and 10% drawdown are slightly different from the results presented in Chapter 10. Here, we utilized the Corporate High Yield Bond Fund Average as reported in the Mutual Fund Expert database of 3/31/2007 from 1979–2007; in Chapter 10, we utilized the data from 1981–2006 on the 22 high yield bond funds listed in Table 10.1.

Chapter 10

[1.] *The New York Times*, August 20, 2006.

[2.] *The New York Times*, "Public Pension Plans Face Billions in Shortages," (August 8, 2006) cited.

[3.] *The New York Times*, "Paying Health Care from Pensions Proves Costly," December 19, 2006.

[4.] *Newsday*.

[5.] *MSN Money*, August 13, 2006, "The death of the retirement safety net."

[6.] *Newsday*, January 2, 2007.

[7.] *New England Journal of Medicine*, January 7, 1999.

[8.] *The New York Times*, "Your Master Card or Your Life," Bob Herbert, January 22, 2007.

[9.] The December 30, 2006, issue of *Newsday* featured an article, "Thinking of Retiring Completely? Think Again," by Saul Friedman.

[10.] *Newsday*, January 13, 2007, "Finding Yourself in Retirement."

INDEX